OECD Urban Studies

The Circular Economy in Valladolid, Spain

This document, as well as any data and map included herein, are without prejudice to the status of or sovereignty over any territory, to the delimitation of international frontiers and boundaries and to the name of any territory, city or area.

Please cite this publication as:
OECD (2020), *The Circular Economy in Valladolid, Spain*, OECD Urban Studies, OECD Publishing, Paris, *https://doi.org/10.1787/95b1d56e-en*.

ISBN 978-92-64-67423-3 (print)
ISBN 978-92-64-81355-7 (pdf)

OECD Urban Studies
ISSN 2707-3432 (print)
ISSN 2707-3440 (online)

Photo credits: Cover: © Getty Images

Corrigenda to publications may be found on line at: *www.oecd.org/about/publishing/corrigenda.htm*.
© OECD 2020

The use of this work, whether digital or print, is governed by the Terms and Conditions to be found at *http://www.oecd.org/termsandconditions*.

Preface

We are very proud to introduce the results of an 18-month policy dialogue with 50+ stakeholders to shape a vision and strategy for a circular economy in the city of Valladolid, Spain as part of the OECD Programme on the Circular Economy in Cities and Regions.

In the face of megatrends such as population growth in cities, urbanisation and climate change, the transition to a circular economy is becoming an imperative for cities of all sizes to reduce the pressure on natural resources, while addressing new infrastructure, services and housing needs, and boosting economic growth and environmental quality. Cities and regions are at the core of citizen well-being, in areas such as transport, solid waste, water or energy.

Moving from a "take-make-dispose" linear system to one in which resource waste is prevented, implies going beyond solely technical aspects and ensure governance and economic conditions are met. For the circular economy to materialise, policies need to be aligned, stakeholders engaged, and legal and regulatory frameworks enabling innovation.

This report summarises important milestones achieved so far. Its analytical framework puts People, Firms and Places at the centre of the shift towards a circular economy. It puts forward bold recommendations and concrete actions for Valladolid to act as promoter, facilitator and enabler of this transition. This requires political leadership and commitment towards the transition to sustainable pathways, as well as multi-stakeholder and multi-sectoral approaches, and new business models.

An important part of the work was the bottom-up and inclusive policy dialogue, whereby each stakeholder could share experience, listen and learn from each other, and benefit from expertise and guidance from peer cities and the OECD team.

While we are aware that we are just at the beginning of the transition from a linear to a circular economy in Valladolid, the city is committed to implement these recommendations and raise their profile within our community and globally. The OECD Centre for Entrepreneurship, SMEs, Regions and Cities stands ready to support Valladolid with this endeavour. This will be all the more relevant in the aftermath of the COVID-19 crisis, when cities and regions will be urged to reconsider the link between environment and health, reflect on the de-materialisation of the economy and society and on circular resources loops in response to the hyper-globalisation of the recent years. The OECD Programme on the Circular Economy in Cities and Regions will seek further opportunities, evidence and recommendations to make the circular economy part of the solution towards healthier, less resource wasteful and environmental aware societies.

Lamia Kamal-Chaoui

Director, OECD Centre for Entrepreneurship, SMEs, Regions and Cities

Oscar Puente

Mayor, City of Valladolid

Ayuntamiento de
Valladolid

Foreword

The circular economy is about preventing wasted resources through reusing materials, improving design to increase the durability of goods and products, and transforming waste.

Population growth, climate change and urbanisation are likely to increase the pressure on natural resources, as well as the demand for new infrastructure, services and housing. By 2050, the global population will reach 9 billion people, 70% of which will be living in cities. Cities represent almost two-thirds of global energy demand, produce up to 80% of greenhouse gas emissions and 50% of global waste.

Cities and regions play a fundamental role in shifting from a linear to a circular economy, as they are responsible for key decisions in local public services such as transport, solid waste, water and energy that affect citizens' well-being, economic growth and environmental quality. In cities and regions, the circular economy should ensure that:

- *services* (e.g. from water to waste and energy) are provided while preventing waste generation, making efficient use of natural resources as primary materials, optimising their reuse and allowing synergies across sectors;
- *economic activities* are planned and executed in a way to close, slow and narrow loops across value chains, and;
- *infrastructure* is designed and built to avoid linear locks-in, which use resources intensively and inefficiently.

The OECD Programme on the Circular Economy in Cities and Regions was designed to support national and subnational governments in their transition towards the circular economy through evidence-based analysis, multi-stakeholder dialogues, tailored recommendations and customised action plans. The Programme relies on a consortium of cities and countries engaged in peer-to-peer dialogues and knowledge sharing activities, including Glasgow (United Kingdom), Granada (Spain), Groningen (Netherlands), Umeå (Sweden), Valladolid (Spain) and Ireland.

This report summarises the findings from an 18-month policy dialogue with the city of Valladolid, Spain to develop a vision for the circular economy transition and learn from existing best practices. Since 2017, transitioning towards the circular economy has been a political priority for Valladolid with the objective of creating new socio-economic opportunities, especially by enhancing innovation in business. The city was one of the first signatories of the *Declaration of Seville* alongside other Spanish municipalities in 2017, and developed a *Circular Economy Roadmap* in 2018. Concretely, Valladolid has granted over one million euros to 61 circular economy related projects promoted by private companies, not-for-profit organisations or research centres.

The report argues that a circular economy strategy in Valladolid could help enhance coherence across existing initiatives, while scaling them up. To that effect, it recommends leveraging the potential of co-ordination across SMEs, local government and university, and considering a more pro-active role of the Agency of Innovation and Economic Development in promoting and facilitating circular economy initiatives.

Acknowledgements

This report was prepared by the OECD Centre for Entrepreneurship, SMEs, Regions and Cities (CFE) led by Lamia Kamal-Chaoui, Director, as part of the Programme of Work and Budget of the Regional Development Policy Committee. It is the result of an 18-month policy dialogue with 50+ stakeholders from public, private, non-profit sectors as well as representatives from the national government, the autonomous community of Castile and Leon and the municipality of Valladolid, Spain.

The report and underlying policy dialogues were co-ordinated by Oriana Romano, Head of the Water Governance and Circular Economy Unit, under the supervision of Aziza Akhmouch, Head of the Cities, Urban Policies and Sustainable Development Division in the CFE. The report was drafted by a core OECD team of experts comprised of Oriana Romano, Luis Cecchi, Policy Analyst and Ander Eizaguirre, Junior Policy Analyst. Special thanks are conveyed to Marco Bianchini, Policy Analyst in the SME and Entrepreneurship Division in CFE, for his participation in the fact-finding mission, inputs and comments on earlier drafts.

The OECD Secretariat is grateful to the Mayor of Valladolid, Mr. Oscar Puente Santiago, for his high level of commitment and leadership towards circular economy in the city. Warm thanks are also extended to the admirable local team in Valladolid led by Rosa Huertas Gonzalez, Director of the Innovation, Economic Development, Employment and Trade Department for the excellent collaboration throughout the dialogue, in particular Jesús Gómez Pérez, Manager of the Agency of Innovation and Economic Development; Luisa María Herrero Cabrejas, Project Manager; Ana Isabel Page Polo, Coordinator of Economic Promotion and Employment; Amparo Ricote Muñoz, Project Manager; Gloria San José Fernández, Project Manager; and Alicia Villazán Cabero, Project manager. Special thanks are also due to Ms. Rosario Chavez López, Councillor for Innovation, Economic Development, Employment and Trade of Valladolid, and Mr. Antonio Gato, Councillor for Finance, Administration and Economic Development (2015-2019).

Furthermore, the policy dialogue benefited from insights from peer reviewers who are warmly thanked for sharing their valuable expertise and city experience, participating in the case study missions and providing international best practices as well as guidance on the report, namely: Eveline Jonkhoff, Program Manager on the Circular Economy and Strategic advisor, (Amsterdam, Netherlands); Aline Otten, Economic Affairs Manager (Groningen, Netherlands); Liv Öberg, Development Strategist (Umeå, Sweden), and Karin Söderström, Sustainability Manager at Vakin water and waste company (Umeå, Sweden).

This report builds on a series of interviews with 50+ stakeholders during the OECD visits to Valladolid (25-28 February 2019 and 29 October 2019) (Annex C), as well as insights from the OECD Survey on the Circular Economy in Cities and Regions and desk research. Interim findings and progress results were presented at the "Workshop: Circular Economy in Cities" during the 40th meeting of the Regional Development Policy Committee (5 November 2018, Paris, France), and at the 1st OECD Roundtable on Circular Economy in Cities and Regions (4 July 2019, Paris, France).

The draft report benefited from written comments by stakeholders engaged throughout the policy dialogue, in particular: Milagros Aguado Mariscal (Trade and Services Federation of Valladolid and Province, FECOSVA), Ana Atienza Pérez (Chamber of Commerce, Industry and Services of Valladolid), Maribel

Barrante (Valladolid Business and Professionals Association, EDUCA), Enrique Cobreros García (Innovative Business Cluster on Efficient Construction, AEICE), José María de Cuenca (AquaVall), Jesús Díez (Natural Heritage of Castile and León Foundation), Carmen Durán (Ministry for Ecological Transition and Demographic Challenge, MITECO), Gonzalo Franco (Workers Commissions, CCOO), Gonzalo Parrado (University of Valladolid), Gema Prieto (Vitartis), Andrés Herguedas, (Valladolid Municipality), Beatriz Quintana Vega (Cultura Circular), Javier Rodríguez Conde (Ecomarketing), Ignacio Rodríguez Muñoz (Duero Hydrographic Confederation), Isabel Tennenbaum Casado (Ecoembes), Dunia Virto González (Foundation of the University School of Agricultural Technical Engineering, INEA), and Juan Carlos Zamora (Energética Cooperative).

The report was submitted to RDPC delegates for approval by written procedure by 6 March 2020 under the cote [CFE/RDPC/URB(2020)3]. The final version was edited and formatted by Eleonore Morena, and François Iglesias and Pilar Philip prepared the manuscript for publication.

Table of contents

Preface	3
Foreword	4
Acknowledgements	5
Abbreviations and acronyms	10
Executive summary	13
1 Towards a circular economy in Valladolid, Spain	**15**
Introduction: The circular economy in cities and regions	16
The drivers for the circular transition in Valladolid, Spain	18
Socioeconomic data and trends	19
Overview of environmental data and trends	21
References	23
Notes	26
2 Assessing and unlocking the circular economy in Valladolid, Spain	**27**
An ongoing agenda on the circular economy at the national level	28
Circular initiatives in the Castile and León Autonomous Community	34
Circular economy initiatives in Valladolid, Spain	35
The analytical framework	38
People and firms: A circular community-enhancing innovation	40
Policies: Identifying sectors holding potential for the circular economy	42
Places: Fostering urban-rural synergies for the circular economy	50
Governance challenges to design and implement the circular transition	52
References	56
Notes	60
3 Policy recommendations and actions for a circular economy in Valladolid, Spain	**63**
Introduction	64
Promoting a vision and a strategy for the circular economy	65
Facilitating multilevel co-ordination for the circular economy	74
Enabling the economics and governance conditions for the uptake of the circular economy	77
References	82

Annex A. Circular economy award-winning projects in 2017 and 2018   85

Annex B. Evaluation criteria applied to select the winning-award projects in 2019   89

Annex C. List of stakeholders consulted during the policy dialogue   91

FIGURES

Figure 1.1. Tag cloud on the circular economy in Valladolid, Spain	18
Figure 1.2. Map of the Castile and León Autonomous Community and Valladolid, Spain	19
Figure 1.3. Share of the working-age population in Valladolid, Spain, 2005-18	20
Figure 1.4. Share of the elderly population in Valladolid, Spain, 2005-18	20
Figure 1.5. Per capita household waste generation in Valladolid, Spain 2008-18	22
Figure 2.1. The circular economy in cities and regions and Sustainable Development Goals	32
Figure 2.2. OECD analytical framework: Level of advancement, tools and roles	38
Figure 2.3. Circularity within and across sectors	42
Figure 2.4. Sectors of interest for a circular economy strategy in Valladolid, Spain	43
Figure 2.5. Waste hierarchy in the EU	48
Figure 3.1. Stakeholders map in Valladolid, Spain	65

TABLES

Table 2.1. Indicators for monitoring the Spanish Circular Economy Strategy	30
Table 2.2. SDG 12 targets and indicators	32
Table 2.3. OECD indicators for a territorial approach to SDG12	33
Table 2.4. The Circular Economy Roadmap: Objectives and actions	37
Table 2.5. Example of sectors included in circular economy initiatives at the subnational level	45
Table 3.1. Policy recommendations for the circular economy in Valladolid, Spain	64
Table 3.2. Circular economy initiatives at the subnational level	66
Table 3.3. OECD Circular Economy Scoreboard for Cities and Regions	81

BOXES

Box 1.1. Examples of circular economy definitions	16
Box 2.1. The Spanish Circular Economy Strategy process	28
Box 2.2. The circular economy in cities and regions and Sustainable Development Goals	31
Box 2.3. Financing instruments for the circular economy: International practices	35
Box 2.4. Circular economy initiatives by the Ecoembes	46
Box 2.5. The EU's approach to waste management	47
Box 2.6. The Castile and León's Bio-Economy Strategy and the Municipal Food Strategy	51
Box 2.7. Examples of economic instruments for the circular economy	54
Box 3.1. City approaches to circular jobs	69
Box 3.2. Examples of labelled products for the circular economy	73
Box 3.3. The proposed OECD Circular Economy Scoreboard for Cities and Regions	81

Follow OECD Publications on:

http://twitter.com/OECD_Pubs

http://www.facebook.com/OECDPublications

http://www.linkedin.com/groups/OECD-Publications-4645871

http://www.youtube.com/oecdilibrary

http://www.oecd.org/oecddirect/

Abbreviations and acronyms

ACEF	Amsterdam Climate and Energy Fund
AEICE	Innovative Business Cluster for Efficient Construction (*Asociación Empresarial Innovadora para la Construcción Eficiente*)
AMA	Amsterdam Metropolitan Area
AMB	Barcelona Metropolitan Area (*Área Metropolitana de Barcelona*)
ARPSI	Areas of Significant Potential Flood Risk (*Áreas de Riesgo Potencial Significativo de Inundación*)
AUE	Spanish Urban Agenda (*Agenda Urbana Española*)
AUVASA	Valladolid City Buses (*Autobuses urbanos de Valladolid*)
AVEBIOM	Spanish Association for Energy Recovery from Biomass (*Asociación Española de Valorización Energética de la Biomasa*)
CCOO	Workers Commissions (*Comisiones Obreras*)
CFE	Centre for Entrepreneurship, SMEs, Regions and Cities
CGPROTEC	Management Consultants and Technological Projects (*Consultores de Gestión y Proyectos Tecnológicos*)
CHD	Duero Hydrographic Confederation (*Confederación Hidrográfica del Duero*)
CO_2	Carbon dioxide
COP	Conference of the Parties
CTR Valladolid	Valladolid's Waste Treatment Centre (*Centro de Tratamiento de Residuos de Valladolid*)
CUVA	Urban Community of Valladolid (*Comunidad Urbana de Valladolid*)
CVE	Business Confederation of Valladolid (*Confederación Vallisoletana de Empresarios*)
EC	European Commission
EFSI	European Fund for Strategic Investments
EIB	European Investment Bank
ELU	Logistic Urban Spaces (*Espaces Logistiques Urbains*)
EPBD	Energy Performance of Buildings Directive
ERDF	European Regional Development Fund
EU	European Union
FECOSVA	Trade and Services Federation of Valladolid and Province (*Federación de Comercio y Servicios de Valladolid y Provincia*)
FEMP	Spanish Federation of Municipalities and Provinces (*Federación Española de Municipios y Provincias*)
FOACAL	Federation of Handicraft Organisations (*Federación de Organizaciones Artesanas de Castilla y León*)
GDP	Gross domestic product
GHG	Greenhouse gas
IAEG	Inter-Agency and Expert Group
ICEX	Institute of Foreign Trade
ICT	Information and communications technology
ILO	International Labour Organization
INEA	University School of Agricultural Engineering (*Escuela Universitaria de Ingeniería Agrícola*)
INFODEF	Institute for Development Promotion and Training (*Instituto para el Fomento del Desarrollo y la Formación*)
ITACYL	Technological Agricultural Institute of Castile and León (*Instituto Tecnológico Agrario de Castilla y León*)

JCYL-FPN	Natural Heritage Foundation Castile and León (*Fundación Patrimonio Natural de Castilla y León*)
LCA	Life Cycle Analysis
LWARB	London Waste and Recycling Board
NECP	National Energy and Climate Plan
NO2	Nitrogen dioxide
NZEB	Nearly Zero Energy Building
O3	Ozone
OECD	Organisation for Economic Co-operation and Development
OVAM	Public Waste Agency of Flanders
PM2.5	Particulate matter smaller than 2.5 microns in diameter
PM10	Particulate matter smaller than 10 microns in diameter
PRAE	Centre of Environmental Resources (*Centro de Recursos Ambientales*)
R&D	Research and development
RCCAVA	Valladolid City Council Air Pollution Control Network (*Red de Control de la Contaminación Atmosférica del Ayuntamiento de Valladolid*)
RDPC	Regional Development Policy Committee
RECI	Spanish Network of Intelligent Cities (*Red Española de Ciudades Inteligentes*)
RISN	Resource Innovation and Solutions Network
SCP	Sustainable consumption and production
SDGs	Sustainable Development Goals
SEMINCI	International Film Week of Valladolid (*Semana Internacional de Cine de Valladolid*)
SEPE	Public Employment Service (*Servicio Público de Empleo Estatal*)
SME	Small- and medium-sized enterprise
SO2	Sulphur dioxide
TL2	Territorial Level 2
UGT	General Union of Workers (*Unión General de Trabajadores*)
UN	United Nations
UVa	University of Valladolid (*Universidad de Valladolid*)
VAT	Value-added tax
VITARTIS	Agro-food Industry Cluster (*Asociación de la Industria Alimentaria de Castilla y León*)

Executive summary

In Valladolid, Spain, the transition to a circular economy is an opportunity for greater attractiveness and competitiveness, while also responding to environmental challenges. In the face of a shrinking and ageing population, combined with significant unemployment (11% in 2018) Valladolid has prioritised the circular economy in the city's strategy to create jobs and stimulate innovation. The city aims to become sustainable city of reference through concrete measures, such as reducing waste, lowering the use of raw materials, increasing the use of renewable energy, while stimulating economic growth and social well-being.

Valladolid was one of the first cities to sign to the *Declaration of Seville* in March 2017 as a follow-up to the "Call to Cities for the Circular Economy" launched in Paris in 2015 during COP 21. Alongside 300 Spanish municipalities, it committed to strengthen the role of local governments in the circular transition by developing local strategies on zero landfill, recycling (especially bio-waste), waste prevention (particularly food waste), eco-design, and public procurement of green products.

Those declarations of intentions have translated into tangible actions. In 2017 and 2018, the municipality launched two calls for projects to finance circular economy initiatives to stimulate local businesses and entrepreneurial activities and raise awareness. The resulting 61 projects received one million euros, which stimulated more applications in the 2019 edition. In follow-up, the Agency of Innovation and Economic Development developed a "Circular Economy Roadmap" for the city, co-organised "Circular Weekends" for networking, and set up a "Circular Lab" to promote an entrepreneurial culture on the circular economy. All these activities helped create a dynamic community of entrepreneurs, micro and small businesses, and civil society acting as ambassadors for the circular economy in Valladolid. Through concrete initiatives related to new business models, eco-design, certifications for circular economy-related industrial processes, platforms connecting supply and demand of secondary material, this community is showing that the transition from a linear to a circular economy is possible and real.

Going forward, moving from an "experimental phase" to a full-fledge transition towards the circular economy will require overcoming a number of challenges:

- **Fostering policy coherence, integration and long-term vision** of existing circular economy-related initiatives to avoid isolated and small-scale actions and maximise synergies across municipal departments and cross-fertilisation;
- **Scaling-up the projects after the experimentation phase** to ensure that projects currently carried out at neighbourhood or individual scale can deliver the expected social, economic and environmental outcomes;
- **Upgrading the skills of authorities** to support their capacity to cope with the complexity of the circular economy. Given the multi-disciplinary nature of the circular economy, the municipality should assess whether the needs of the circular economy transition matches the skills and human resources available within municipality departments and take action to bridge identified gaps;
- **Improving the data, knowledge and information base** on the circular economy to generate understanding and awareness of companies and citizens on the potential benefits of the circular

economy. This could also facilitate stakeholder engagement, monitoring and evaluation for greater trust and accountability.

The report recommends concrete actions to improve Valladolid's ability to promote, facilitate and enable the circular economy. In particular:

- **To promote the circular economy**, the municipality could:
    - identify priorities based on the analysis of material flows and production and consumption trends;
    - develop a circular economy strategy with clear vision and objectives, while accounting for opportunities for job creation;
    - lead by example through applying circular principles in the municipality's activities and services;
    - strengthen the circular community, creating spaces for meetings and dialogues, and;
    - raise awareness on the circular economy by showing successful business cases and making circular products and services recognisable through labels, which could be also an incentive for local business.
- **To facilitate collaboration among a wide range of actors** to make the circular economy happen on the ground, the municipality could
    - coordinate with national and regional circular economy strategies;
    - foster collaborations across universities, business, and citizens, and exchange experiences with neighbouring cities;
    - support business development and stimulate entrepreneurship in the circular economy.
- **To enable the necessary governance and economic conditions**, the municipality could:
    - identify the regulatory, fiscal and economic tools incentivising the circular economy and develop capacity building tools for municipal personnel and entrepreneurs;
    - strengthen the role of the Agency of Innovation and Economic Development as a municipal focal point and facilitator;
    - implement green public procurement initiatives;
    - facilitate the sharing of tools and initiatives among neighbours for small-scale initiatives as a step for local change, and identify areas for experimentation;
    - strengthen the effectiveness of the municipal grants related to the circular economy, and;
    - develop a monitoring and evaluation framework with specific indicators on the circular economy to analyse progress and results.

1 Towards a circular economy in Valladolid, Spain

This chapter provides an overview on the circular economy in cities and focuses on the rationale for the circular economy transition in the city of Valladolid, Spain, by looking at main drivers leading to a shift from a linear to a circular economy, and socioeconomic and environmental data and trends.

Introduction: The circular economy in cities and regions

The transition to a circular economy is underway and cities and regions are at the centre of it. By 2050, the global population will reach 9 billion people, 70% of which will be living in cities (UN, 2018[1]). The pressure on natural resources will increase, while new infrastructure, services and housing will be needed. Already, cities represent almost two-thirds of global energy demand (IEA, 2016[2]) and produce up to 80% of greenhouse gas emissions (World Bank, 2010[3]). By 2050, urban dwellers will still be the most exposed to high concentrations of air pollutants[1] (OCDE, 2012[4]). Cities produce 50% of global waste (UNEP, 2013[5]). It is estimated that globally, by 2050, the levels of municipal solid waste will double (IEA, 2016[2]; UNEP/IWSA, 2015[6]). A total of 80% of food is consumed in cities and compared to today's levels, 60% more food will be required in the coming decades to feed the population (Ellen MacArthur Foundation, 2019[7]). At the same time, water stress and water consumption will increase by 55% by 2050 (OCDE, 2012[4]). Cities and regions have core responsibilities for local public services such as transport, solid waste, water and energy. As such, they are at the centre of key decisions having a strong impact on citizens' well-being, environmental quality and economic growth.

There is no unique definition for circular economy, which is now facing a validity challenge period. Although there are many definitions of the circular economy, they all include as a basic assumption the recognition of waste as a resource (Box 1.1). The circular economy is about preventing wasted resources through reusing materials, improving design to increase the durability of goods and products, and transforming waste. In cities and regions, the circular economy should ensure that: *services* (e.g. from water to waste and energy) are provided whilst preventing waste generation, making efficient use of natural resources as primary materials, optimising their reuse and allowing synergies across sectors; *economic activities* are planned and carried out in a way to close, slow and narrow loops across value chains and *infrastructure* is designed and built to avoid linear locks-in, which use resources intensively and inefficiently.

The circular economy is not an end per se, but a means to an end: it provides an opportunity to do more with less, to better use available natural resources and to transform waste into new resources, while promoting new jobs opportunities and tackling inequalities (e.g. access to sharing services and commodities, form mobility to agro-food, to buildings). As such, while the environmental narrative, whereby less use of materials implies reduced greenhouse gas (GHG) emissions has been so far predominant in promoting the shift to a circular economy, cities and regions are increasingly paying attention to the social and the economic aspects, as drivers for this transition. According to Blomsma and Brennan (2017[8]), the circular economy is now facing its "validity challenge period" on its way to becoming a robust and consolidated concept, implying a radical shift in consumer behaviour.

> **Box 1.1. Examples of circular economy definitions**
>
> - "The circular economy is where the value of products, materials and resources is maintained in the economy for as long as possible, and the generation of waste minimised." (EC, 2015[9])
> - "The circular economy is restorative and regenerative by design. Relying on system-wide innovation, it aims to redefine products and services to design waste out while minimising negative impacts. A circular economy is then an alternative to a traditional linear economy (make, use, dispose)." (Ellen MacArthur Foundation, 2018[10])
> - "An economic system that replaces the end-of-life concept, with reducing, alternatively using, recycling and recovering materials in production/distribution and consumption processes. It operates at the micro level (products companies, consumers), meso level (eco-industrial parks) and macro level (city, region, nation and beyond), with the aim of accomplishing sustainable development, thus simultaneously creating environmental quality, economic prosperity and

> social equity, to the benefit of current and future generations. It is enabled by novel business models and responsible consumers." (Kirchherr, Reike and Hekkert, 2017[11])
>
> - "The circular economy is one that has low environmental impacts and that makes good use of natural resources, through high resource efficiency and waste prevention, especially in the manufacturing sector, and minimal end-of-life disposal of materials." Ekins et al. (2019[12])
>
> - "There are three different layers of circularity, with increasingly broad coverage: i) closing resource loops; ii) slowing resource loops; and iii) narrowing resource loops. All these explicitly or implicitly aim at addressing the market failures associated with materials use, the failure to address local environmental consequences associated with extraction; or the failure to include the environmental externalities associated with waste generation. Furthermore, there are economic inefficiencies associated with the inefficient use of scarce resources." (OECD, 2019[13]).
>
> Source: EC (2015[9]), *Closing the Loop – An EU Action Plan for the Circular Economy*, https://eur-lex.europa.eu/legal-content/EN/TXT/HTML/?uri=CELEX:52015DC0614&from=EN (accessed on 21 February 2020); Ellen McArthur Foundation (2018[10]), *What is a Circular Economy?*, https://www.ellenmacarthurfoundation.org/circular-economy/concept (accessed on 21 February 2020); Kirchherr, J., D. Reike and M. Hekkert (2017[11]), "Conceptualizing the circular economy: An analysis of 114 definitions", http://dx.doi.org/10.1016/j.resconrec.2017.09.005; Ekins et al. (2019[12]), "The Circular Economy: What, Why, How and Where", Background paper for an OECD/EC Workshop on 5 July 2019 within the workshop series "Managing environmental and energy transitions for regions and cities", Paris; OECD (2019[13]), *Global Material Resources Outlook to 2060: Economic Drivers and Environmental Consequences*, https://doi.org/10.1787/9789264307452-en.

The circular economy in cities and regions is expected to generate a positive impact on economic growth, the creation of new jobs and the reduction of negative impacts on the environment. By 2030, shifting from a linear approach of "take, make and dispose" to a circular system is estimated to hold a potential of USD 4.5 trillion for economic growth (Accenture, 2015[14]). Projections show that, by 2030, resource productivity in Europe can improve by 3% and generate a gross domestic product (GDP) increase of up to 7% (McKinsey Centre for Business and Environment, 2016[15]). Projections at the city level show that for example, applying a circular economy approach to the construction chain in the city of Amsterdam (Netherlands) would decrease GHG emissions by half a million tonnes of CO_2 per year. In London (United Kingdom), the benefits from circular approaches applied to the built environment, food, textiles, electricals and plastics are estimated at GBP 7 billion every year by 2036.[2] About 50 000 jobs related to the circular economy are estimated to be created in the Île-de-France region.[3] Environmental benefits consist of: decreased pollution; increased share of renewable or recyclable resources; and reduced consumption of raw materials, water, land and energy (EEA, 20016[16]). Yet, the transition should be "just" by taking into account people' social well-being, quality of life and equity.

The potential of the circular economy still needs to be unlocked. Today, less than 10% of the global economy is circular (Circle Economy, 2020[17]). Unlocking the potential of the circular economy in cities and regions implies going beyond solely technical aspects and putting the necessary governance in place to create incentives (legal, financial), stimulate innovation (social, institutional) and generate information (data, knowledge, capacities). It would also mean looking at the barriers for businesses to "close the loops", by re-thinking business models (e.g. leasing and sharing) and analysing the economic instruments that could support the transition in several sectors, including waste, food, built-up environments and water. The circular economy implies governance models based on multi-stakeholder and multi-sectoral approaches. For the circular economy to happen, policies need to be aligned, stakeholders informed and engaged, legal and regulatory frameworks updated and in support of innovation.

The drivers for the circular transition in Valladolid, Spain

For the city of Valladolid, Spain, the transition to a circular economy represents an opportunity for greater attractiveness and competitiveness, while providing responses to environmental challenges. Figure 1.1 indicates the words that the city through the OECD Survey on the Circular Economy in Cities and Regions most associates with the circular economy concept (the bigger the word in the figure, the higher the importance). These words are: "sustainable development", "climate change", "efficiency", "business model" and "cultural change". According to the local administration, waste prevention, eco-design and recycling are key for the circular economy (OECD, 2019[18]). In particular, the city aims to maximise the use of natural resources, such as agro-food resources, promote the industrial symbiosis and improve separate waste collection for recycling and materials' valorisation. This implies fostering public awareness and participation, enhancing innovation and promoting co-operation amongst stakeholders (Puente, 2018[19]).

Figure 1.1. Tag cloud on the circular economy in Valladolid, Spain

Note: The respondent had to choose the top 5 words most often associated with the circular economy. The answer is based on the following question: "Please indicate the top 5 words from the list suggested below you most often associate with circular economy in your context, ranking from 1 (most important) to 5 (less important)".
Source: Own elaboration based on the city of Valladolid's answers to the OECD (2019[18]) OECD Survey on the Circular Economy in Cities and Regions.

Since adhering to the Declaration of Seville in March 2017, the city of Valladolid has showed political willingness towards a circular transition. Valladolid was one of the first cities to adhere to the Declaration of Seville in March 2017, which followed the Call to Cities for the Circular Economy launched in Paris in September 2015 on the occasion of COP 21. Through the Declaration of Seville, 300 Spanish municipalities committed to promoting a sustainable, inclusive and resilient urban development model and strengthening the role of local governments in the circular transition by developing local strategies on: zero landfills; recycling (especially bio-waste); waste prevention (particularly food waste); eco-design; and public procurement of green products. Although not binding, the declaration represents a starting point for Spanish municipalities to take action towards a circular economy. Following the signature, the Agency of Innovation and Economic Development of the municipality of Valladolid started drafting a Circular Economy Roadmap and the Department of Innovation, Economic Development, Employment and Trade made available municipal grants for circular projects (see next paragraphs).

The Spanish Circular Economy Strategy and a series of initiatives at the subnational level fostered the development of circular economy models in Valladolid. Although not yet approved, the Spanish Circular

Economy Strategy (Government of Spain, 2018[20]) is a reference for subnational governments willing to transition from a linear to a circular economy, including for Valladolid. The strategy serves as a general framework that can be adopted and implemented by regional and local governments according to their specific competencies and priorities (see Chapter 2). Beyond the national reference, other initiatives stimulated a fertile environment for planning the transition to a circular economy in the city of Valladolid. For example, the municipality actively participated in the development of the "Circular economy local strategy model" by the Spanish Federation of Municipalities and Provinces (*Federación Española de Municipios y Provincias*, FEMP). Moreover, the municipality shares information with Castile and León Autonomous Community for the elaboration of its Circular Economy Strategy 2020-30.

The participation of the city of Valladolid in several projects funded by the European Commission (EC) led the municipality to conceive the circular economy as an umbrella framework for sustainable development projects. The municipality of Valladolid is actively engaged in a series of EC funded projects promoting sustainable urban development, through energy efficiency, district heating, sustainable mobility, and nature-based solutions.[4] These projects stimulated new forms of public-private collaborations and enhanced environmental awareness. As such, lessons learnt from the practice of the EC funded projects (e.g. communication, budget management, partnerships, etc.) are intended to be used to implement the future circular economy strategy of the city, since multi-stakeholder collaborations (across public, private and not-for-profit sectors, academia, local associations and citizens) will be needed.

Socioeconomic data and trends

Valladolid is the most populated city of the Castile and León Autonomous Community. Castile and León (2 425 801 inhabitants in 2018) is the sixth most populated region in the country (Castile and León Autonomous Community, 2018[21]) and the most extensive in territorial terms, although population density is low with 25.5 inhabitants per km2 (EC, 2019[22]). The region is located in the northern half of the country (Figure 1.2). A total of 12% of the region's inhabitants and 57% of the province's population live in the city of Valladolid (INNOLID 2020+, 2017[23]). In 2018, the population amounted at 298 866 inhabitants, mostly concentrated in the historical centre, but increasingly moving to less densely populated and peripheral areas of the city. Four peripheral districts (Numbers 4, 6, 10 and 11) of a total of 12 city districts concentrate 78% of the population (Valladolid en Cifras, 2019[24]).

Figure 1.2. Map of the Castile and León Autonomous Community and Valladolid, Spain

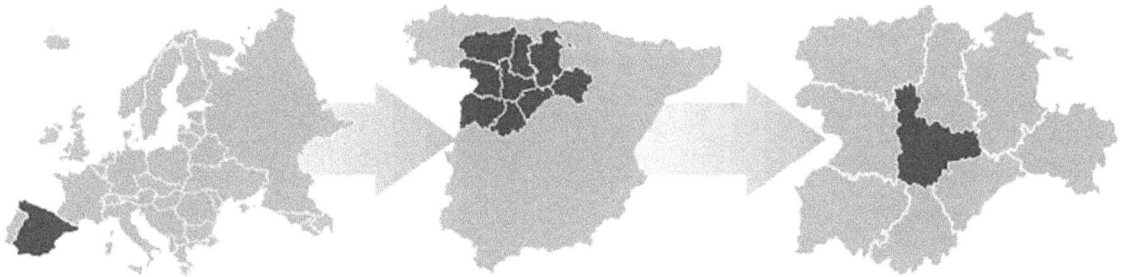

Source: Webpage of Valladolid Municipality (2020[25]), *Cómo llegar - Portal de Cultura y Turismo de Valladolid*, https://www.info.valladolid.es/como-llegar.

The population of the city of Valladolid has been shrinking and ageing during the last two decades and this trend is projected to continue during the next decade. Since 1998, the municipality of Valladolid has lost almost 7% of its population. During the last 5 years, the provincial population has dropped by 2%. This is due to death rates rising above the number of new-borns and the net balance between emigrants and immigrants (almost 1 000 in 2017) (INE, 2019[26]). Some neighbouring municipalities have absorbed the excess of emigrants from the capital, becoming "dormitory towns". Between 2005 and 2018, the working population decreased by almost 10% (Figure 1.3) and, among it, the 25-34 age group was the one which decreased the most. During the same period, the youth index[5] decreased from 67% to 45.8%, while the ageing index shows that the senior population (over 64) grew almost 10% (Figure 1.4).

Figure 1.3. Share of the working-age population in Valladolid, Spain, 2005-18

16-64 year-olds

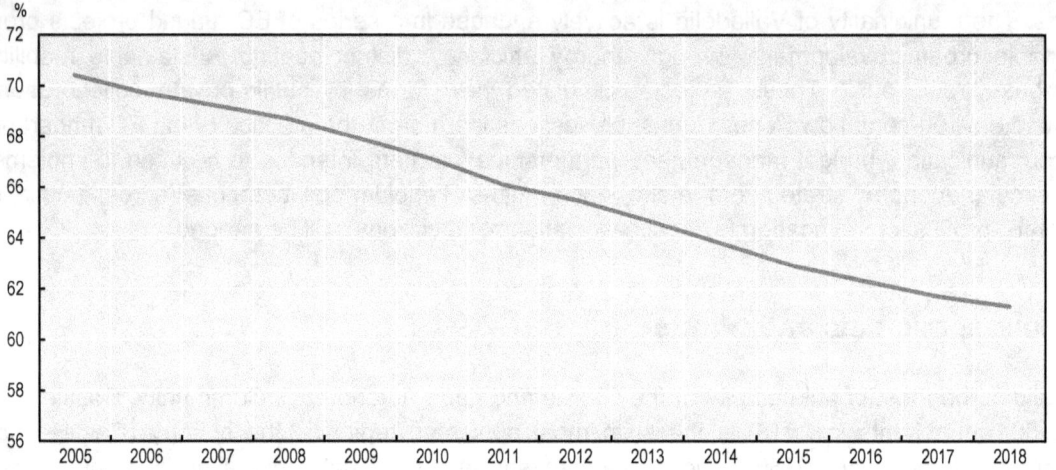

Source: Own elaboration based on Valladolid en Cifras (2019[24]), *Homepage*, http://www.valladolidencifras.es/ (accessed on 11 June 2019).

Figure 1.4. Share of the elderly population in Valladolid, Spain, 2005-18

+65 year-olds

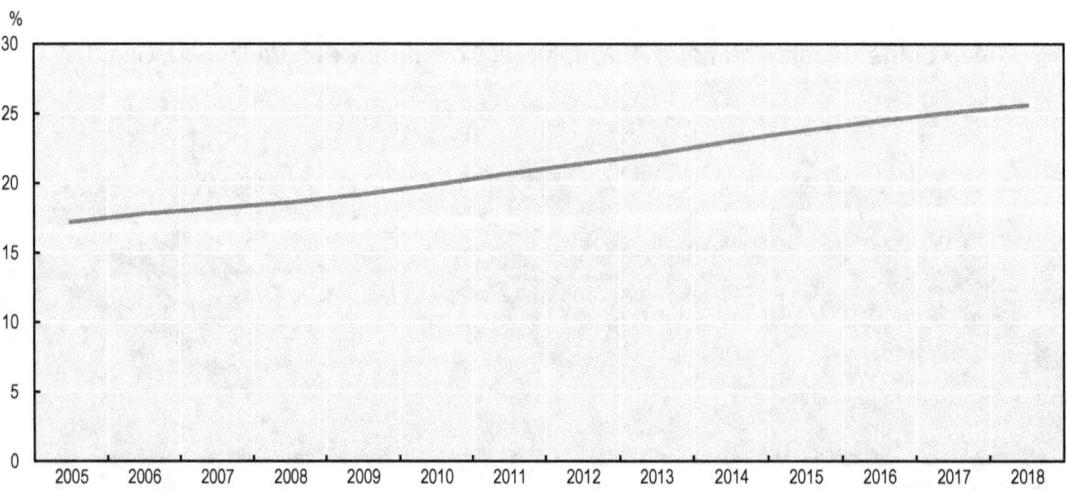

Source: Own elaboration based on Valladolid en Cifras (2019[24]), *Homepage*, http://www.valladolidencifras.es/ (accessed on 11 June 2019).

Valladolid's economy is characterised by the service sector. A total of 83% of existing firms in the city operates in the service sector, followed by the construction (11%), industrial (almost 5%) and agriculture sectors (less than 1%) (INNOLID 2020+, 2017[23]). The GDP of the metropolitan area of Valladolid and that of the region are equivalent respectively to almost 1% and 5% of the national GDP (OECD, 2019[27]). In 2016, the GDP per capita in the province of Valladolid was EUR 24 308, slightly above the regional value (EUR 22 646) and the national level (EUR 23 970) (INE, 2016[28]).[6] Valladolid hosts big international firm subsidiaries, such as Michelin and Renault.[7] However, the productive sector is mainly characterised by small- and medium-sized enterprises (SMEs), as in the whole region. In Castile and León, a total of 90% of companies are SMEs and 83% of them have less than 3 salaried workers (EC, 2019[22]).

Unemployment in Valladolid has been decreasing since 2014 and is lower than the regional and national levels. Since the financial crisis in 2008, unemployment has been a great concern in Spain. At the beginning of the crisis, in 2008, unemployment represented 9.6%. By 2013, it had almost tripled to a maximum of 26.9% and started to fall until reaching 13.8% in 2019. This figure is almost 2 times higher than the EU average of 7.5% (Eurostat, 2019[29]). In the city of Valladolid, the level of unemployment[8] has increased from 7.8% to 15.7% between 2008 and 2014 and has been fluctuating, reaching 11.7% in 2018 (Valladolid Municipality, 2019[30]). Unemployment in the city highly affects individuals above 25 years old (40.8% of this group age) and above 45 years old (49.3%) (INNOLID 2020+, 2017[23]). A total of 9.9% of youth under 25 years old are unemployed and a total of 27% of young professionals leave the city after ending their studies (INNOLID 2020+, 2017[23]). In order to attract "brains", the municipality launched a talent return programme, offering two-year grants and a talent retention programme to incentivise local companies hiring recent graduates from the University of Valladolid for a six-month internship (Valladolid Municipality, 2018[31]).

The tourist sector is gaining increasing relevance, due to the rich cultural heritage of the city and the presence of international events. Valladolid was home to historical iconic figures such as Christopher Columbus, who died in Valladolid in 1506, and Miguel de Cervantes, whose first edition of "Don Quixote" was published in Valladolid in 1604. Since 1965, the city has been hosting the International Film Week of Valladolid (SEMINCI), attracting each year around 95 000 visitors. Valladolid is the most visited city in Castile and León with almost 455 926 visitors in 2018 (INE, 2019[26]), corresponding to 1.4% increase in visitors compared to the year 2017 (INE, 2018[32]). In 2017, the tourism sector generated EUR 277 million, almost 18% more than in 2016, creating 4 639 jobs (16% more than the previous year) (INNOLID 2020+, 2017[23]).

The city hosts one of the oldest universities in Spain. The University of Valladolid, founded in 1346, has four campuses located in the municipalities of Palencia, Segovia, Soria and Valladolid. The School of Industrial Engineering was ranked, in 2016, as the seventh-best in Spain for the link between the competencies acquired by students and the required skills for a career in the business sector (Everis Foundation, 2016[33]). The university is also known for its School of Architecture.

Overview of environmental data and trends

Air pollution has been decreasing since 2002, although it is still an issue for the city. Since 2008, the number of days reporting "bad" and "regular" atmospheric quality has dropped sensibly, whereas days considered as "good" and "very good" have increased. Carbon emissions in Valladolid have decreased by 8% since 2010 (Interreg Europe, 2019[34]). The municipality, following the Anti-pollution Protocol (*Protocolo de Anticontaminación de Valladolid*), adopted limitations to traffic in the city centre on seven occasions during 2017 to reduce air pollution levels. The Atmospheric Pollution Control Network (*Red de Control de Contaminación Atmosférica del Ayuntamiento de Valladolid*, RCCAVA) has 5 quality air monitoring stations located throughout the city that measure the level of particles (PM10, PM2.5) and other gases (NO_2, O_3, SO_2, CO_2). The municipality attributes air pollution to the extensive use of private vehicles and is taking measures for greener mobility through European funds (INNOLID 2020+, 2017[23]).

Renewable energy production has been increasing although it remains at low levels compared to traditional energy sources. Biogas and thermal solar energy (local) have been the predominant renewable energy sources since the beginning of the 2000s up to 2014. The municipal thermal solar energy has kept a similar production level throughout that period. Photovoltaic and biomass, while almost inexistent at the beginning of the analysed period, have seen a big increase between 2010 and 2014 (INNOLID 2020+, 2017[23]).

Household waste per capita production stands below regional and national values; however, fluctuations have been registered in recent years. Nowadays, a total of each 380 kg of waste per household per year are produced in Valladolid, below the regional value of 433 kg and the 459 kg generated in Spain. The per capita household waste production has increased by almost 8% since 2014 (when it was 353 kg/inhabitant), after showing a decreasing trend between 2011 and 2014 (Figure 1.5). The downward trend might be due, amongst others, to the slowdown in consumption associated with the 2008 international crisis (Lomas and Carpintero, 2017[35]). Household waste separation levels amounted at 40% of the total waste produced between 2010 and 2018 (Valladolid Municipality, 2019[36]). Total municipal waste production has increased between 2002 and 2010 from approximately 115 000 tonnes to 128 000 tonnes. Since then and until 2014, the production of waste has dropped up to its minimum (108 000 tonnes) (CTR Valladolid, 2018[37]). Since 2014, municipal waste production has remained relatively stable although, in the last 3 years, the amount of total waste has increased by 2% (reaching 113 212 tonnes in 2018) (Valladolid Municipality, 2019[36]).

Figure 1.5. Per capita household waste generation in Valladolid, Spain 2008-18

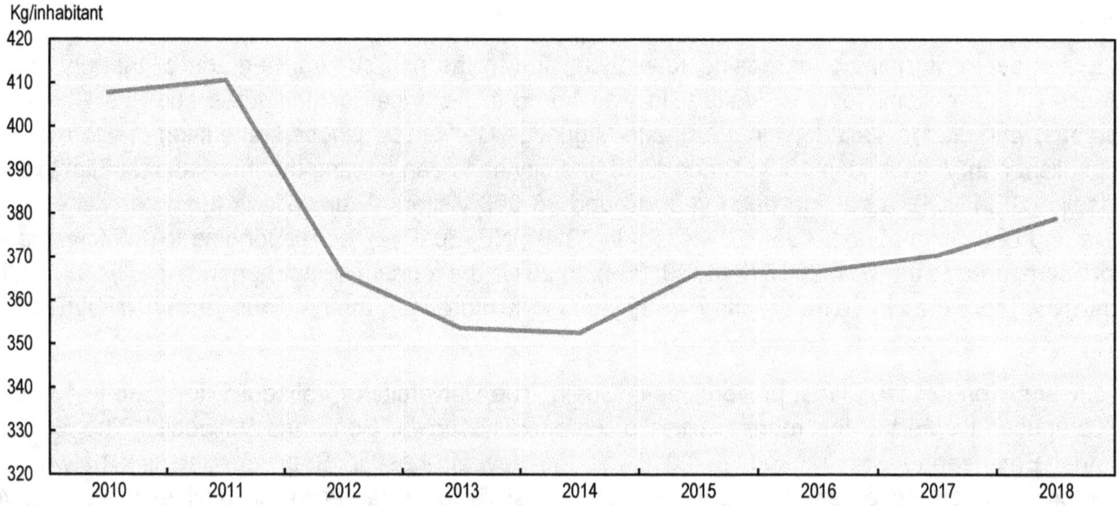

Source: CTR Valladolid (2018[38]), *Datos del CTR*, http://www.ctrvalladolid.com/datos-ctr (accessed on 3 August 2019).

Household water consumption shows a downward trend since 2004. Litres of water consumed per capita per day (l/pc/d) in Valladolid have been slightly falling, from about 300 l/pc/d in 2004 to 260 l/pc/d in 2018. This figure shows a 5% reduction compared to 2017 and the city's projections for 2019 were expecting to keep the same trend reaching 255 l/pc/d (although data for 2019 are not yet available). The municipality attributes this reduction to increased awareness and citizen engagement campaigns (INNOLID 2020+, 2017[23]). On the other hand, water consumed for irrigation of parks and gardens has increased by 150% since 2000, driven, partly, by the increase of green areas surface in the city (Valladolid Municipality, 2018[39]).

The city is exposed to the risks of flooding. Valladolid is part of the Pisuerga-Esgueva Area of Potential Significant Flood Risk (*Áreas de Riesgo Potencial Significativo de Inundación*, ARPSIs). Between 2009 and 2013, floods have caused damages equivalent, on average, to EUR 1 506 255 per year (Duero Hydrographic Confederation, 2016[40]).

References

Accenture (2015), "The circular economy could unlock $4.5 trillion of economic growth", https://newsroom.accenture.com/news/the-circular-economy-could-unlock-4-5-trillion-of-economic-growth-finds-new-book-by-accenture.htm (accessed on 21 February 2020). [14]

Blomsma, F. and G. Brennan (2017), "The emergence of circular economy: A new framing around prolonging resource productivity", *Journal of Industrial Ecology*, Vol. 21/3, pp. 603-614, http://dx.doi.org/10.1111/jiec.12603. [8]

Castile and León Autonomous Community (2018), *Estadística Junta de Castilla y León*, https://estadistica.jcyl.es/web/jcyl/Estadistica/es/Plantilla100/1246989275272/_/_/_ (accessed on 29 November 2019). [21]

Circle Economy (2020), *The Circularity Gap Report*, https://docs.wixstatic.com/ugd/ad6e59_733a71635ad946bc9902dbdc52217018.pdf. [17]

CTR Valladolid (2018), *Datos del CTR*, http://www.ctrvalladolid.com/datos-ctr (accessed on 3 August 2019). [38]

CTR Valladolid (2018), *Entradas de residuos en el año 2018*, http://www.ctrvalladolid.com/assets/datos/2018.pdf (accessed on 3 August 2019). [37]

Duero Hydrographic Confederation (2016), *Plan de Gestión del Riesgo de Inundación*, https://www.chduero.es/pgri-plan-de-gestion-del-riesgo-de-inundacion (accessed on 21 October 2019). [40]

EC (2019), *EURES - Labour Market Information - Castilla y León*, European Commission, https://ec.europa.eu/eures/main.jsp?countryId=ES&acro=lmi&showRegion=true&lang=en&mode=text&regionId=ES0&nuts2Code=%20&nuts3Code=null&catId=440 (accessed on 31 May 2019). [22]

EC (2015), *Closing the Loop – An EU Action Plan for the Circular Economy*, European Commission, https://eur-lex.europa.eu/legal-content/EN/TXT/HTML/?uri=CELEX:52015DC0614&from=EN (accessed on 21 February 2020). [9]

EEA (20016), *Environmental Indicator Report 2016 - In Support to the Monitoring of the 7th Environment Action Programme*, European Environment Agency, https://www.eea.europa.eu//publications/environmental-indicator-report-2016 (accessed on 21 February 2020). [16]

Ekins, P., Domenech, T., Drummond, P., Bleischwitz, R., Hughes, N. and Lotti, L. (2019), *"The Circular Economy: What, Why, How and Where"*. Background paper for an OECD/EC Workshop on 5 July 2019 within the workshop series "Managing environmental and energy transitions for regions and cities", Paris. [12]

Ellen MacArthur Foundation (2019), *Cities and Circular Economy for Food*, https://www.ellenmacarthurfoundation.org/assets/downloads/Cities-and-Circular-Economy-for-Food_280119.pdf (accessed on 6 November 2019). [7]

Ellen MacArthur Foundation (2018), *What is a Circular Economy?*, https://www.ellenmacarthurfoundation.org/circular-economy/concept (accessed on 21 February 2020). [10]

Eurostat (2019), *Unemployment Statistics - Statistics Explained*, https://ec.europa.eu/eurostat/statistics-explained/index.php/Unemployment_statistics (accessed on 29 November 2019). [29]

Everis Foundation (2016), *La UVA, entre las diez mejores de España en Ciencias e Ingeniería*, El Norte de Castilla, https://www.elnortedecastilla.es/valladolid/201607/04/entre-diez-mejores-espana-20160704115228.html (accessed on 1 August 2019). [33]

Government of Spain (2018), *España Circular 2030, Estrategia Española de Economía Circular*, Gobierno de España, http://www.miteco.gob.es/images/es/180206economiacircular_tcm30-440922.pdf (accessed on 31 May 2019). [20]

IEA (2016), "Cities are in the frontline for cutting carbon emissions", https://www.iea.org/news/cities-are-in-the-frontline-for-cutting-carbon-emissions-new-iea-report-finds (accessed on 21 February 2020). [2]

INE (2019), *Viajeros y pernoctaciones por comunidades autónomas y provincias*, Spanish Statistical Office Website, http://www.ine.es/jaxiT3/Datos.htm?t=2074 (accessed on 11 June 2019). [26]

INE (2018), *Contabilidad regional de España (Últimos datos)*, https://www.ine.es/dyngs/INEbase/es/operacion.htm?c=Estadistica_C&cid=1254736167628&menu=ultiDatos&idp=1254735576581 (accessed on 1 August 2019). [43]

INE (2018), *Viajeros y pernoctaciones por comunidades autónomas y provincias*, http://www.ine.es/jaxiT3/Tabla.htm?t=2074 (accessed on 1 August 2019). [32]

INE (2016), *Contabilidad regional de España - Producto Interior Bruto regional*, https://www.ine.es/prensa/cre_2016_1.pdf (accessed on 1 August 2019). [28]

INNOLID 2020+ (2017), *Estrategia de desarrollo urbano, sostenible e integrado para la ciudad de Valldolid*, http://www.valladolidadelante.es/node/12063 (accessed on 11 June 2019). [23]

Interreg Europe (2019), *Sustainable Energy Action Plan (SEAP)*, Interreg Europe, https://www.interregeurope.eu/ (accessed on 3 August 2019). [34]

Kirchherr, J., D. Reike and M. Hekkert (2017), "Conceptualizing the circular economy: An analysis of 114 definitions", *Resources, Conservation and Recycling*, Vol. 127, pp. 221-232, http://dx.doi.org/10.1016/j.resconrec.2017.09.005. [11]

Lomas, P. and O. Carpintero (2017), *Metabolismo y Huella ecológicade la alimentación: El caso de Valladolid (Diagnóstico para la Estrategia Alimentaria Local)*, http://www.alimentavalladolid.info/wp-content/uploads/2017/11/Metabolismo-Alimentario-Valladolid_definitivo.pdf (accessed on 21 October 2019). [35]

McCarthy, A., R. Dellink and R. Bibas (2018), "The Macroeconomics of the Circular Economy Transition: A Critical Review of Modelling Approaches", *OECD Environment Working Papers*, No. 130, OECD Publishing, Paris, https://dx.doi.org/10.1787/af983f9a-en. [41]

McKinsey Centre for Business and Environment (2016), *Growth Within: A Circular Economy Vision for a Competitive Europe*. [15]

OCDE (2012), *OECD Environmental Outlook to 2050: The Consequences of Inaction*, OECD Publishing, Paris, https://doi.org/10.1787/9789264122246-en. [4]

OECD (2019), *Global Material Resources Outlook to 2060: Economic Drivers and Environmental Consequences*, OECD Publishing, Paris, https://dx.doi.org/10.1787/9789264307452-en. [13]

OECD (2019), *OECD Metropolitan Explorer*, http://www.oecd.org/cfe/regional-policy/regionalstatisticsandindicators.htm. [27]

OECD (2019), *OECD Survey on the Circular Economy in Cities and Regions*, OECD, Paris. [18]

Puente, O. (2018), *Interview to the Mayor of Valladolid, Óscar Puente*, http://www.municipiosyeconomiacircular.org/entrevistas/2018/3/5/oscar-puente-alcalde-de-valladolid (accessed on 31 May 2019). [19]

UN (2018), "68% of the world population projected to live in urban areas by 2050", United Nations, http://www.un.org/development/desa/en/news/population/2018-revision-of-world-urbanization-prospects.html (accessed on 6 November 2019). [1]

UNEP (2013), *UNEP-DTIE Sustainable Consumption and Production Branch*. [5]

UNEP/IWSA (2015), *Global Waste Management Outlook*. [6]

Valladolid en Cifras (2019), *Homepage*, http://www.valladolidencifras.es/ (accessed on 11 June 2019). [24]

Valladolid Municipality (2020), *Cómo llegar - Portal de Cultura y Turismo de Valladolid*, https://www.info.valladolid.es/como-llegar. [25]

Valladolid Municipality (2019), *Datos de empleo. Ayuntamiento de Valladolid*. [42]

Valladolid Municipality (2019), *Gestión de residuos. Ayuntamiento de Valladolid*. [36]

Valladolid Municipality (2019), *Valladolid en Cifras Website*, http://www.valladolidencifras.es/ (accessed on 11 June 2019). [30]

Valladolid Municipality (2018), *Evolución del Consumo de Agua de Riego en los Parques y Jardines de Valladolid*. [39]

Valladolid Municipality (2018), *Subvenciones para el retorno del talento al municipio de Valladolid*, http://www.valladolid.es/es/ciudad/innovacion-desarrollo/ayudas-subvenciones/subvenciones-retorno-talento-municipio-valladolid-2018 (accessed on 11 June 2019). [31]

World Bank (2010), *World Development Report 2010*, World Bank, http://dx.doi.org/10.1596/978-0-8213-7987-5. [3]

Notes

[1] Air pollutant concentrations refer in particular to Particulate Matter (PM10).

[2] Amec Foster Wheeler: see focus area profiles in this document (pp. 20-30) (2015), https://www.lwarb.gov.uk/wp-content/uploads/2015/12/LWARB-circular-economy-report_web_09.12.15.pdf.

[3] For more information, see: https://www.paris.fr/economiecirculaire.

[4] The REMOURBAN project promotes electric mobility and buildings' energy efficiency (e.g. in the FASA district in *Las Delicias* neighbourhood). The Urban Green Up project, which will be executed until 2023, provides nature-based solutions towards a more resilient city.

[5] The share of population younger than 15 years old in relation to the population older than 64.

[6] Available data for 2018 shows the following GDP values: Castile and León (EUR 24 397) and Spain (EUR 25 854) (INE, 2018[43]).

[7] The automotive sector counts 42 companies based in the Province including big international firms subsidiaries (Iveco, Michelin and Renault) which create 14 000 direct jobs and produce EUR 7 million a year on average (INNOLID 2020+, 2017[23]).

[8] At the municipal level, unemployment data is calculated considering the number of unemployed workers registered under the Public Employment Service (*Servicio Público de Empleo Estatal*, SEPE) in relation to the working population (between 16 and 64 years old) (Valladolid Municipality, 2019[42]).

2 Assessing and unlocking the circular economy in Valladolid, Spain

The chapter details the main components of the existing circular economy strategies and initiatives promoted by the Spanish Government, Castile and León Autonomous Community and the city of Valladolid, Spain. The chapter also identifies actors, policies and co-operation tools across urban and rural areas that can foster the circular economy. Finally, it describes the main challenges the city of Valladolid is facing in its transition from a linear to a circular economy.

An ongoing agenda on the circular economy at the national level

The Spanish Circular Economy Strategy to 2030 (*España Circular 2030*) was developed in 2018 but has not yet been approved. The Spanish Circular Economy Strategy (2018[1]) was jointly promoted in 2018 by the Ministry of Agriculture and Fisheries, Food and the Environment *(Ministerio de Agricultura, Pesca y Alimentación)* and the Ministry of Economy, Industry and Competitiveness *(Ministerio de Economía y Competitividad)*. An inter-ministerial commission formed by nine ministries[1] and the Economic Office of the President at that time contributed to it, together with the autonomous communities and the Spanish Federation of Municipalities and Provinces (FEMP). After the election in November 2019, the inter-ministerial committee added new ministries (e.g. the Ministry of Education and Vocational Training, *Ministerio de Educación y Formación Profesional*) to the nine previous ones, while each ministry faced organisational changes in their areas of responsibility.[2] The strategy has a long-term vision that is expected to be implemented through short-term action plans, enabling the required adjustments to complete the transition by 2030 (Box 2.1). The National Action Plan for 2019-20 attached to the strategy foresees a budget of EUR 630 million for 4 thematic areas (production and design; consumption; waste management; secondary materials and water reuse) and 3 cross-cutting areas (awareness and participation; research and development; and employment and training) (Government of Spain, 2018[1]).

Box 2.1. The Spanish Circular Economy Strategy process

A key step for the development of the national strategy on the circular economy was the Pact for a Circular Economy, engaging the main economic and social stakeholders in Spain in circular business models. The pact was the result of a workshop organised in 2017 by the Ministries of Agriculture and Fisheries, Food and Environment and of Economy, Industry and Competitiveness. It gathered European Union (EU) officials, national, regional and city-level representatives, institutions specialised in the circular economy and civil society organisations (Government of Spain, 2018[1]). By September 2019, a total of 347 stakeholders adhered to the pact. Adherence remains open to new stakeholders.

The signatory party of the Pact for a Circular Economy committed to boost the transition to a circular economy through ten actions:

1. Reduce the use of non-renewable resources and promote the reuse of secondary materials.
2. Foster product life cycle analysis and eco-design.
3. Promote the application of the principles of the waste hierarchy.
4. Advance innovation and efficiency in production processes.
5. Encourage sustainable consumption patterns.
6. Endorse a responsible consumption model through transparency measures and eco-labels.
7. Establish institutional channels to create synergies between public administrations, the scientific community and economic and social stakeholders.
8. Disseminate the importance of transitioning towards a circular economy.
9. Promote the use of common indicators to measure the grade of advancement of the circular economy.
10. Include social and environmental impact indicators derived from the companies' actions.

In 2018, following the pact, the Spanish Circular Economy Strategy incorporated almost 2 000 observations from autonomous communities, the Spanish Federation of Municipalities and

> Provinces (FEMP) and citizens. A circular economy inter-ministerial commission was created during the elaboration process of the strategy. It is planned that the inter-ministerial commission will continue to meet at least once a year to evaluate and monitor the implementation of the national strategy. The inter-ministerial commission created a working group for autonomous communities responsible for forming other working groups to further implement the strategy. Lastly, one of the actions of the Declaration of Climate Emergency (*Acuerdo de Consejo de Ministros por el que se aprueba la Declaración del Gobierno ante la emergencia climática y ambiental*), approved by the Spanish Government in January 2020, calls to "to promote the circular economy in economic sectors and economic and industrial processes and to adopt the Circular Economy Strategy and a Waste Law that will address, among other issues, the problem of single-use plastics, in order to achieve the "zero residue" goal on the 2050 horizon."
>
> Source: Government of Spain (2018[1]), *España Circular 2030, Estrategia Española de Economía Circular*, http://www.miteco.gob.es/images/es/180206economiacircular_tcm30-440922.pdf (accessed on 31 May 2019); Ministry for Ecological Transition and the Demographic Challenge (2018[2]), *Información pública de la estrategia Española de Economía Circular*, https://www.miteco.gob.es/es/calidad-y-evaluacion-ambiental/participacion-publica/Residuos-2018-Nota-sobre-proceso-informacion-publica-estrategia-espanola-economia-circular.aspx; Government of Spain (2020[3]) *Acuerdo de Consejo de Ministros por el que se aprueba la Declaración del Gobierno ante la emergencia climática y ambiental*, https://www.miteco.gob.es/es/prensa/declaracionemergenciaclimatica_tcm30-506551.pdf (accessed 26 February 2020); Ministry for Ecological Transition and the Demographic Challenge (2020[4]), *El Gobierno declara la emergencia climática*, https://www.miteco.gob.es/es/prensa/200121cmindeclaracionemergencia_tcm30-506549.pdf (accessed 20 February 2020).

The Spanish Circular Economy Strategy reflects the objectives of the EU Circular Economy Package and identifies priority sectors (Box 2.5). The national strategy has 12 general strategic objectives and aims to reduce by 30% the national consumption of materials in relation to the gross domestic product (GDP) by 2030, taking 2015 as the reference year. A specific objective of increasing material efficiency (e.g. reducing raw materials used during production) has been incorporated in 2019. The government focuses on five sectors: construction, agro-food, industry, tourism and consumer goods. Strategy's results will be monitored and evaluated through indicators that reflect those defined by the EU, in order to enhance consistency between the two approaches. Furthermore, eight specific indicators, corresponding to the areas of the National Action Plan, complete the monitoring system. These indicators concern: production and consumption; secondary raw materials; repair, reuse and recycle; water reuse taxation; research, innovation and competitiveness; participation and awareness; and employment and training (Table 2.1).

The Spanish National Urban Agenda includes the promotion of the circular economy as one of its ten strategic objectives. The Spanish Urban Agenda (*Agenda Urbana Española*, AUE) is a strategic voluntary document, which pursues the achievement of sustainability in urban development policies in Spain, promoted by the Ministry of Development in 2019 (2019[5]). The fourth objective of the Spanish Urban Agenda consists of "sustainable management of resources and favouring the circular economy" (Ministry of Development, 2019[5]). Currently, EUR 1 362 million from the urban axis of the European Regional Development Fund (ERDF) in Urban Sustainable and Integrated Development Strategies are available to finance projects related to Strategic Objectives of the Spanish Urban Agenda, including favouring the circular economy (Ministry of Development, 2019[5]). In 2020, the Ministry of Transport, Mobility and the Urban Agenda and the Spanish Federation of Municipalities and Provinces (FEMP) created a permanent forum of cities (*Foro Ciudades*) for bilateral meetings between national and local governments on the Urban Agenda.

Table 2.1. Indicators for monitoring the Spanish Circular Economy Strategy

Objective	Indicator	Description	Last available value and unit of measure
Production and design			
Reduce the use of raw materials in production processes, promoting recycling, repairable materials, minimising the introduction of harmful substances and driving the economy in a more sustainable and efficient way	Material productivity	GDP per unit of domestic material consumption	EUR 2.745/tonne
Consumption			
Reduce the ecological footprint by fostering responsible consumption habits to avoid food waste and reduce non-renewable raw material consumption	Domestic material consumption	Quantity of material used directly in the economy	402 789 351 thousands of tonnes
Waste management			
Apply the waste hierarchy effectively to boost prevention, reduction, reuse and recycling	Recycling rate	Result of dividing recycling waste into treated waste in percentage	37.1% (mass)
Secondary raw materials commerce			
Guarantee the protection of the environment and human health by reducing natural non-renewable resources consumption and reintroducing secondary materials in the production process	Balance of recycling raw materials commerce	Export-import of waste and by-products	-3 989 tonnes
Reused water			
Promote efficient water use to allow the protection of quality and quantity of water bodies with sustainable and innovative harnessing	Volume of reused water	Volume of regenerated residual water used for industry, watering gardens, sports centres and recreation areas, sewage and street cleaning, and other uses	1 453 995 m3/day
Research, innovation and competitiveness			
Promote the development and application of new knowledge, technology and innovation in processes, services, business models, fostering public-private collaboration and promoting private investment in research, development and innovation (RDI)	Patents related to recycling and secondary raw materials as a proxy for innovation	Number of patents registered in recycling and secondary raw materials	28.65 patents
Participation and awareness			
Promote economic and social entities involvement, in general, and citizens, in particular, to raise awareness of present environmental, economic and technology challenges and the need for the general application of waste hierarchy	Number of circular economy signatories	Number of signatories of the Circular Economy Pact	55 signatories
Employment and training			
Promote the creation of new jobs and improve existing ones in a circular economy framework	Number of circular economy jobs		..

Source: Government of Spain (2018[1]), *España Circular 2030, Estrategia Española de Economía Circular*, http://www.miteco.gob.es/images/es/180206economiacircular_tcm30-440922.pdf (accessed on 31 May 2019).

In order to guide municipalities and provinces towards the transition to a circular economy, the Spanish Federation of Municipalities and Provinces (FEMP) developed a Circular Economy Local Strategy Model

(*Modelo de estrategia local de economía circular*) (2019[6]). The strategy model is a non-binding document made for and by municipalities and provinces as guidance to advance towards circularity and sustainability in several sectors. The document is strictly linked to the 2030 Agenda for Sustainable Development (Box 2.2). In a decentralised system such as in Spain where there are more than 8 131 municipalities (INE, 2020[7]), each municipality can develop its own sustainability programme, according to its needs and capabilities. The strategy defines four strategic axes of work and identifies cross-cutting areas:

- Use of natural resources: Consists of actions to prevent and reuse secondary materials and of sustainable waste management.
- Water consumption management: Involves optimising the water supply and sewage networks and the reuse of wastewater.
- Urban spaces sustainability: Promotes a preventive and regenerative urban planning approach to recover old city districts, to enhance resilience and energy efficiency and sustainable mobility in order to comply with the EU and World Health Organization standards for air quality.
- Healthy habits and spaces: Aims to foster healthy territories (e.g. rural and urban sustainable development, healthy habits), responsible consumption and the minimisation of food waste.
- Cross-cutting areas: Consist of measures across sustainable and innovative public procurement; development and implementation of new digital technologies; transparency and shared governance; and communication and awareness-raising.

The FEMP's Circular Economy Local Strategy Model provides a self-assessment questionnaire to enable each municipality to measure how advanced it is in terms of circularity. The methodology applied in the strategy starts with a diagnosis stage. This stage consists of a "yes/no" questionnaire listing the strategy's 175 actions detailed in 4 strategic axes and 25 measures. According to the FEMP Circular Economy Local Strategy Model, each municipality, looking at the number of actions that are in place, can evaluate its level of circularity: low (0-1 actions), moderate (2-3 actions), high (4-5 actions), very high (6-7 actions). This diagnosis can be the first step in the elaboration of a circular economy programme at the local level and the design of a monitoring plan (FEMP, 2019[6]).

Box 2.2. The circular economy in cities and regions and Sustainable Development Goals

The 2030 Agenda for Sustainable Development, adopted in 2015 by United Nations (UN) member states, includes 17 Sustainable Development Goals (SDGs). The aim of the 2030 Agenda is to set a 15-year-long plan to end poverty and other deprivations while implementing strategies that improve health and education, reduce inequality, promote economic growth and tackle climate change.

The circular economy is an interesting implementation vehicle to SDG 12, pledging for more sustainable and responsible consumption and production patterns. Moreover, it is relevant for the achievement of SDGs 6 (water), 7 (energy), 11 (sustainable cities and communities), 13 (climate action) and 15 (life on land) (Figure 2.1).

Figure 2.1. The circular economy in cities and regions and Sustainable Development Goals

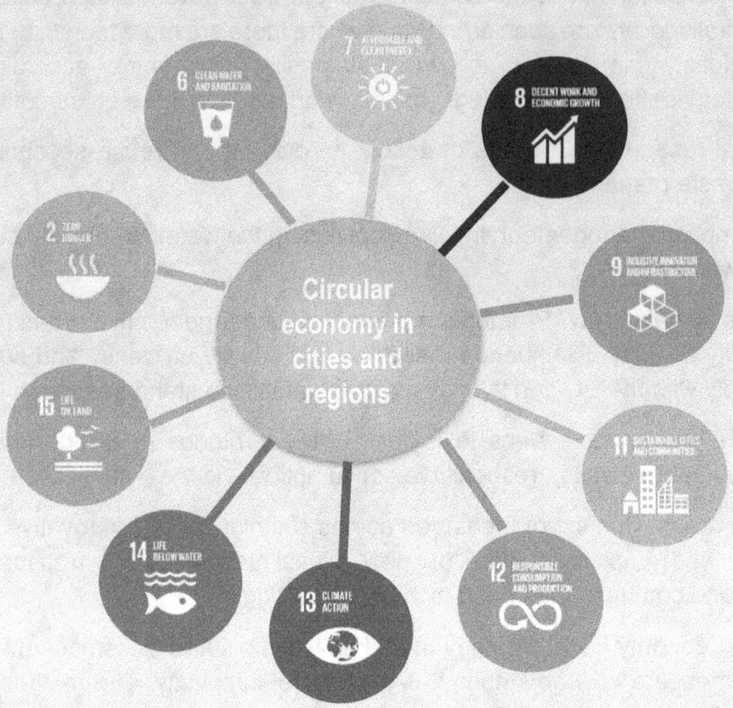

Source: OECD (forthcoming[8]), *The Circular Economy in Cities and Regions*, Synthesis Report, OECD Publishing, Paris.

The SDG 12 is composed of 11 targets and 13 indicators (Table 2.2).

Table 2.2. SDG 12 targets and indicators

	Targets		Indicators
12.1	Implement the 10-year framework of programmes on sustainable consumption and production, all countries taking action, with developed countries taking the lead, taking into account the development and capabilities of developing countries	12.1.1	Number of countries with sustainable consumption and production (SCP) national action plans or SCP mainstreamed as a priority or a target into national policies
12.2	By 2030, achieve the sustainable management and efficient use of natural resources	12.2.1	Material footprint, material footprint per capita, and material footprint per GDP
		12.2.2	Domestic material consumption, domestic material consumption per capita, and domestic material consumption per GDP
12.3	By 2030, halve per capita global food waste at the retail and consumer levels and reduce food losses along production and supply chains, including post-harvest losses	12.3.1	Global food loss index
12.4	By 2020, achieve the environmentally sound management of chemicals and all wastes throughout their life cycle, in accordance with agreed international frameworks, and significantly reduce their release to air, water and soil in order to minimise their adverse impacts on human health and the environment	12.4.1	Number of parties to international multilateral environmental agreements on hazardous waste, and other chemicals that meet their commitments and obligations in transmitting information as required by each relevant agreement
		12.4.2	Hazardous waste generated per capita and proportion of hazardous waste treated, by type of treatment

12.5	By 2030, substantially reduce waste generation through prevention, reduction, recycling and reuse	12.5.1	National recycling rate, tons of material recycled
12.6	Encourage companies, especially large and transnational companies, to adopt sustainable practices and to integrate sustainability information into their reporting cycle	12.6.1	Number of companies publishing sustainability reports
12.7	Promote public procurement practices that are sustainable, in accordance with national policies and priorities	12.7.1	Number of countries implementing sustainable public procurement policies and action plans
12.8	By 2030, ensure that people everywhere have the relevant information and awareness for sustainable development and lifestyles in harmony with nature	12.8.1	Extent to which: i) global citizenship education and ii) education for sustainable development (including climate change education) are mainstreamed in: a) national education policies; b) curricula; c) teacher education; and d) student assessment
12.a	Support developing countries to strengthen their scientific and technological capacity to move towards more sustainable patterns of consumption and production	12.a.1	Amount of support to developing countries on research and development for sustainable consumption and production and environmentally sound technologies
12.b	Develop and implement tools to monitor sustainable development impacts for sustainable tourism that creates jobs and promotes local culture and products	12.b.1	Number of sustainable tourism strategies or policies and implemented action plans with agreed monitoring and evaluation tools
12.c	Rationalise inefficient fossil-fuel subsidies that encourage wasteful consumption by removing market distortions, in accordance with national circumstances, including by restructuring taxation and phasing out those harmful subsidies, where they exist, to reflect their environmental impacts, taking fully into account the specific needs and conditions of developing countries and minimising the possible adverse impacts on their development in a manner that protects the poor and the affected communities.	12.c.1	Amount of fossil-fuel subsidies per unit of GDP (production and consumption) and as a proportion of total national expenditure on fossil fuels

Source: UN (2019[9]), *Goal 12: Sustainable Development Knowledge Platform*, https://sustainabledevelopment.un.org/sdg12 (accessed on 7 February 2020).

The OECD programme "A Territorial Approach to the SDGs" has developed a comprehensive indicator framework to measure where cities and regions stand on their SDG implementation path. Specifically regarding SDG12, the programme has identified three indicators to measure the progress of this goal (Table 2.3).

Table 2.3. OECD indicators for a territorial approach to SDG12

Goal	Indicator description	Subnational scale	Source	Desired direction
SDG 12. Responsible consumption	Municipal waste rate (kilos per capita)	TL2 and Functional urban area (FUA)	OECD Regional Database (TL2) and Eurostat (FUA)	Negative
	Percentage of municipal waste that is recycled	TL2	OECD Regional Database	Positive
	Number of motor road vehicles per 100 people	TL2 and F Functional urban area (FUA)	OECD Regional Database (TL2) and Eurostat (FUA)	Negative

> Note: Functional urban areas are economic units characterised by a city (or core) and a commuting zone that is functionally interconnected to the city. A city is a local administrative unit (i.e. LAU for European countries, such as municipality, local authorities, etc.) where at least 50% of its population live in an urban centre. An urban centre is defined as a cluster of contiguous grid cells of 1 km2 with a density of at least 1 500 inhabitants per km2 and a population of at least 50 000 inhabitants overall.
> The Territorial Level 2 (TL2) in the OECD classification refers to regional administrative regions officially established in each country.
> Source: OECD (2020[10]), *A Territorial Approach to the Sustainable Development Goals: Synthesis report*, https://dx.doi.org/10.1787/e86fa715-en and OECD (2012[11]), *Functional Urban Areas by Country*, https://www.oecd.org/cfe/regional-policy/functionalurbanareasbycountry.htm.
>
> Sources: UN (2019[9]), *Goal 12: Sustainable Development Knowledge Platform*, https://sustainabledevelopment.un.org/sdg12 (accessed on 7 February 2020); OECD (2020[10]), *A Territorial Approach to the Sustainable Development Goals: Synthesis Report*, https://dx.doi.org/10.1787/e86fa715-en.

Circular initiatives in the Castile and León Autonomous Community

Several initiatives are set in the Castile and León Autonomous Community to promote the transition to a circular economy. Since 2015, the circular economy was included as part of the government's programme as a means to boost the regional economy (Castile and León Environment Department, 2018[12]). Afterwards, several initiatives followed:

- Strategy: The Castile and León 2020-30 Circular Economy Strategy is under elaboration. The strategy's elaboration process started in 2016 with the creation of a group of experts and the presentation of a roadmap, which included the following steps: participation structure; analysis of available resources, strategic sectors and actors; identification of needs and existing instruments; actions and monitoring indicators (Castile and León Environment Department, 2018[12]). The region is characterised by three main economic activities: livestock, mining and the bio-economy. The bio-economy has a key role in the strategy as a potential way to replace imported non-renewable materials. Increasing productivity of material use will be key for the region (using less, reusing more). Finally, the strategy presents several objectives related to a change of the economic, productive and consumption models, such as: going beyond waste management solutions; reducing virgin material use, by replacing them by secondary bio-based materials; increasing reuse; promoting local commerce, as one of the main promoters of the circular economy; and advancing in the work through a sectoral approach.
- Research: The regional circular economy strategy identified six priority sectors and four priority action themes for the circular economy. The priority sectors are: agro-food; automotive; health and quality of life; tourism and heritage; energy and environment; and habitat. Priority action themes include: research on eco-innovation; waste as a resource conception; new consumption models; capacity building, awareness and participation; financing; and monitoring and socioeconomic impact measurement (Castile and León Environment Department, 2018[12]). In 2018, Castile and León has included the circular economy in the ongoing EU Research and Innovation Strategies for Smart Specialisation (RIS 3) project. A material flow analysis has been performed despite the lack of proper data indicators at the regional level.
- Capacity building: During 2017-19, the regional training and support programme in research, development and innovation called Centr@tec delivered eight workshops on the circular economy to businesses and entrepreneurs based in the region. The workshops focused on: eco-innovation, new business models, organic matter and bio-economy, waste as a resource, the automotive sector, the building sector, agro-food business opportunities and industry and raw materials (Castile and León Environment Department, 2018[12]). The Natural Heritage Foundation of Castile and León Autonomous Community also organises training on Green Public Procurement (Natural

Heritage of Castile and León, 2018[13]). The "Circular Lab" offers co-working and entrepreneurship spaces in the city of Valladolid, as well as capacity building programmes for entrepreneurs.
- Awareness-raising: A number of initiatives are in place, such as: the "Circular Deals" events, which aim to identify barriers to the circular transition in the regions; and the "Living Lab, which promotes sustainable consumption actions among citizens.

Circular economy initiatives in Valladolid, Spain

In Valladolid, circular economy-related activities are promoted by the Department of Innovation, Economic Development, Employment and Trade and by its technical arm, the Agency of Innovation and Economic Development. The agency's main goals are to promote the city's economic and sustainable development and support employment, entrepreneurship and innovation. Since 2017, the agency is in charge of developing a circular economy's strategic lines of work. The agency considers the transition towards a circular economy key to achieving the goal of reducing waste, while creating new jobs and enhancing innovation (Agency of Innovation and Economic Development, 2019[14]). Since June 2019, the new municipal government has included the definition of a circular economy strategy as one of its 2019-23 programmatic objectives (Agency of Innovation and Economic Development, 2019[14]).

The city of Valladolid promotes circular economy projects through municipal grants. In 2017 and 2018, the municipality launched two calls for projects to finance circular economy initiatives aiming to stimulate local businesses and entrepreneurial activities, while raising awareness on the circular economy. The local government-financed a total of 61 projects (22 and 39 respectively in 2017 and 2018), allocating a budget of EUR 960 000 (EUR 400 000 and EUR 560 000 in 2017 and 2018 respectively). The municipality financed between 40% and 85% of the project's total cost. The beneficiaries of the grants were private companies, associations of private companies, non-profit entities or research centres based in the municipality of Valladolid (Annex A). An additional EUR 600 000 are assigned for 2019-21 (this amount represents 0.17% of the annual budget of the city). The financing rules for the 2019-20 calls have been updated, foreseeing co-funding (10%) by winning projects and a 2-phase grant transfer whereby 80% is granted in the starting phase of the project and the pending 20% is granted after showing the project's results (in previous calls 100% of funding was given at the beginning of the project). Examples of other financing instruments for the circular economy and ongoing related initiatives are illustrated in Box 2.3.

Box 2.3. Financing instruments for the circular economy: International practices

There are several initiatives (at the local, national and international levels) that seek to accelerate the transition to a circular economy by improving access to funding for circular economy projects:

- **Revolving funds**: The city of Amsterdam, Netherlands through the Amsterdam Climate and Energy Fund (ACEF) and the Sustainability Fund invested in more than 65 projects related to climate, sustainability and air quality for a total of EUR 30 million. The revolving funds allow to reinvest revenues within 15 years to fund additional sustainable energy production, energy efficiency or circular economy projects. Each of the funded projects must contribute to the aims of the Sustainability Agenda approved by the City Council in 2015. Regarding the nature of the financing, the ACEF provides funding in the form of loans, warranties and/or share capital, subject to a maximum of EUR 5 million per project.
- **Venture capital and growth capital**: The London Waste and Recycling Board (LWARB) supports circular businesses through the Circular Economy Business Support Programme. The venture capital fund supports circular economy small- and medium-sized enterprises (SMEs) in various steps of start-up financing and in scaling up businesses that are already in the market.

> Moreover, the LWARB, through the Circularity European Growth Fund 1 operated by Circularity Capital, seeks investment opportunities in circular businesses with proven cash flow and profit, which need significant capital to scale up.
>
> - **Loans and funds**: The European Investment Bank (EIB) offers medium- and long-term loans for large scale circular economy projects and indirect financing through local banks and other agents for smaller projects, particularly related to SMEs. Other new circular economy project models can also be financed by the European Fund for Strategic Investments (EFSI),[3] and InnovFin[4]. In 2020, the EIB within the Urban Agenda Partnership for the Circular Economy launched the "Circular City Funding Guide" to provide an overview of available financing tools to cities, businesses and stakeholders wishing to advance towards a circular economy. Different types of financing tools are organised under the following categories: guarantees, equity, debt, grants and alternative funding sources.
>
> - **Bonds**: Private banks are showing an increasing interest in the circular economy transition. In 2019, for the first time, a private Italian bank issued a "sustainable bond" for circular economy projects (EUR 750 million were allocated to this end). A Dutch bank plans to allocate EUR 1 billion in the next 5 years to finance circular projects with the objective of saving 1 million tonnes of CO2 in 5 years. Selected projects receive an initial circular assessment and are guided in the identification of circular opportunities. The network FinanCE, created in 2014, gathers commercial and public banks and institutional investors interested in supporting the circular transition.
>
> Source: C40 Cities (2016[15]), *C40 Good Practice Guides: Amsterdam - Sustainability Fund and Amsterdam Climate and Energy Fund*, http://www.c40.org/case_studies/c40-good-practice-guides-amsterdam-sustainability-fund-and-amsterdam-climate-energy-fund (accessed on 6 June 2019); London Waste and Recycling Board (2019[16]), *London Waste and Recycling Board Website*, http://www.lwarb.gov.uk/ (accessed on 6 June 2019); EC (2019[17]), *Improving Access to Finance for Circular Economy Projects*, http://dx.doi.org/10.2777/983129; EIB (2019[18]), *The EIB Circular Economy Guide: Supporting the Circular Transition*, http://www.eib.org/attachments/thematic/circular_economy_guide_en.pdf (accessed on 2 August 2019); London Waste and Recycling Board (2019[19]), *Circular Economy Investment for Businesses in London*, http://www.lwarb.gov.uk/what-we-do/circular-london/circular-economy-investment-for-businesses/ (accessed on 5 August 2019); OECD (2019[20]), *OECD Highlights of the 1st OECD Roundtable on the Circular Economy in Cities and Regions*, OECD, Paris; Urban Agenda Partnership for Circular Economy (2020[21]), *The Circular City Funding Guide*, European Investment Bank, https://www.circularcityfundingguide.eu/ (accessed on 6 February 2020); OECD (forthcoming[8]), *The Circular Economy in Cities and Regions*, Synthesis Report, OECD, Paris.

To be eligible, circular economy-related projects were requested to create jobs and economic return in the city of Valladolid. Criteria for eligibility were the following: promotion of employment; economic and social dimensions; technical and methodological quality; environmental relevance; eco-innovation and eco-design; innovative character; quantitative and qualitative impact scope; diversification of the supports; and priority products (bio-plastics and food waste). The same criteria were applied for the project selection in the 2019-20 call for grants (detailed in Annex B). However, new aspects such as textile and rubber were incorporated as priority sectors to be considered by applicants, in addition to the previous ones, such as plastics, bio-plastics and food waste. During the first year of the grant in 2017, a total of 23 projects out of 38 were selected. The 15 projects that were not selected did not meet the quality criteria, measured through predefined thresholds. In the second year, in 2018, the number of applications increased up to 60. This was due most probably to greater awareness on the topic, as well as to improved application conditions (e.g. longer period to respond to the call). In 2019, a total of 32 projects were selected from 70 candidate projects.

Circular economy-funded projects in Valladolid concern a number of sectors, such as waste, water and energy. Projects focus on different areas such as: i) education and training, through developing skills and human capital (e.g. artisan practices; workshops and mentoring); ii) dissemination, consisting of raising awareness and bringing the concept of the circular economy into everyday life (e.g. sharing and reuse products and goods); iii) research studies, producing data on the status quo and potential of the circular economy in the city that can inform public policy decisions (e.g. a study on business and citizens' awareness level towards a circular economy or a guide on how the use of recycled waste from the construction and demolition sector can be included in the city's public tenders); and iv) implementation projects, consisting in fostering new technologies (e.g. bioenergy, solar panels, reusing pistachio industry waste), strengthening citizen participation (e.g. an online platform to share experiences) and creating a circular economy community (e.g. mentoring and networking events). An evaluation study on the results of the programme is ongoing, however, the municipality has expressed the need for establishing synergies across projects and scaling them up (Valladolid City Council, 2018[22]).

The municipality fosters the connection between stakeholders through supporting networking events. The Circular Weekend, one of the municipal circular economy grant-awarding projects, consists in a two-day event hosted on the premises of the municipality, to promote peer-learning, launch circular ideas, share existing business models and create a network of people interested in pushing forward the circular economy approach. In the 2017 and 2018 editions, the event hosted almost 100 participants offering presentations, workshops and mentoring sessions. The Circular Weekend has been an opportunity to connect local stakeholders and stimulate new projects. For example, some of the award-winner projects (Annex A) applied to the municipal call for grants after participating in the Circular Weekend. In March 2019, the municipality gathered all the winning projects from 2017 to present their main results and share them with the 2018 winners. The most recent Circular Weekend took place in June 2019 and attracted 50 participants (Valladolid Municipality, 2019[23]).

In 2018, the Agency of Innovation and Economic Development developed a Circular Economy Roadmap for the city of Valladolid, as a result of the experience of municipal grants. The Circular Economy Roadmap sets objectives and related actions (Table 2.4). The roadmap is the result of good practices collected through circular economy projects that benefitted from municipal grants since 2017, as well as from exchanges with other cities and networks (e.g. Covenant of Mayors, Eurocities, Michelin Cities, Spanish Network of Intelligent Cities-RECI, etc.).

Table 2.4. The Circular Economy Roadmap: Objectives and actions

Objectives	Actions
Define the approach	Political support Technical co-operation Cross-cutting approach
Make a diagnosis	Regulatory framework Mapping of flows, stakeholders Data sets Indicators Benchmarking
Raise awareness and encourage participation	Communication plan Workshops, seminars Training programme Call for grants
Promote circular economy among companies, businesses and the entrepreneurial ecosystem	Promotion of entrepreneurship Circular Weekend Circular Lab Call for grants
Position Valladolid as a circular city	City networking International projects and events

Source: Own elaboration based on Valladolid Municipality (2018[24]), *Valladolid Roadmap towards a Circular Economy*.

A Circular Lab aims to build capacities amongst entrepreneurs. In particular, the Circular Lab benefits from exchanges with other cities in Portugal and Spain (Valladolid Municipality, 2019[25]). It provides entrepreneurs and start-ups specialised in circular economy businesses with operational resources (physical spaces, networking, etc.); it helps develop adequate skills and create a favourable attitude among entrepreneurs towards new professional opportunities and business ideas; it promotes the integration of the circular economy in the entrepreneurial culture and innovative ideas in all phases of the value chains, through the creation of new products and processes. The Circular Lab was created in 2019. It is managed by the Agency of Innovation and Economic Development of the City of Valladolid. Further, another Circular Lab is managed by the Natural Heritage Foundation of Castile and León Autonomous Community. Circular labs are EU-funded projects. In addition, the local government grants awards to bachelor's and master's thesis that focus on ten topics that the city identified as strategic, including the circular economy.

The analytical framework

The analytical framework used in this report is based on three dimensions that help to identify tailored solutions for cities and regions willing to transition from a linear to a circular economy (Figure 2.2):

- The level of advancement of cities and regions in the transition to a circular economy: Advanced, In progress, Newcomers.
- Tools and instruments for the transition according to the 3Ps Framework: People, Policies and Places.
- Roles of cities and regions to promote, facilitate and enable the circular economy.

Figure 2.2. OECD analytical framework: Level of advancement, tools and roles

Source: OECD (forthcoming[8]), *The Circular Economy in Cities and Regions*, Synthesis Report, OECD Publishing, Paris.

According to the level of advancement towards the transition to a circular economy, it is possible to identify three clusters of cities and regions:

- **Advanced**: Cities and regions that have developed and put in place circular economy strategies. These cities show strong innovative initiatives, as well as a firm political will in favour of a circular economy. An important future priority for these cities would be to build metrics for measuring progress and evaluating their policies in place. Brussels and the Flanders region (Belgium), Paris (France), Amsterdam (Netherlands) and London (United Kingdom) belong to this cluster.

- **In progress**: Cities "in progress" are those that are taking actions towards the circular economy, following ad hoc initiatives. Cities or regions in this cluster have recently set specific programmes on the circular economy and/or are starting their implementation. They are less advanced compared to the pioneers, but they have already taken key steps towards a circular economy. This is the case of Rotterdam (Netherlands), the Metropolitan Area of Barcelona (Spain) and Glasgow (United Kingdom), amongst others.

- **Newcomers**: Cities in this cluster recognise the relevance and potential of the circular economy and they are exploring options for implementation. These cities have already achieved good results in waste recycling levels (Oslo, Norway); water reuse (Granada, Spain); have signed political commitments to advance towards a circular economy (Milan and Prato, Italy); are starting to develop a circular economy strategy (Groningen, Netherlands; Umeå, Sweden); or have included the circular economy in broader policy plans (Helsinki and Oulu, Finland). These cities see in the circular economy a means for reducing environmental impacts in cities while increasing attractiveness and competitiveness. The city of Valladolid is included in this cluster.

Each city and region, regardless of their level of advancement, can identify the conditions needed to transition to a circular economy, making sure that *people* are engaged, *policies* are co-ordinated and that linkages across *places* are set to close the loops (3Ps Framework) (OECD, 2016[26]):

- **People**: The circular economy is a shared responsibility across levels of government and stakeholders. As such, it is key to identify the actors that can play a role in the transition and allow the needed cultural shift towards different production and consumption pathways, new business and governance models. For example, the business sector can determine the shift towards new business models (e.g. renting, reusing, sharing, etc.). Citizens, on the other hand, make constant consumption choices and can influence production.

- **Policies**: The circular economy requires a holistic and systemic approach that cuts across sectoral policies. As somebody's waste can be a resource for somebody else, the circular economy provides the opportunity to foster complementarities across policies. The variety of actors, sectors and goals makes the circular economy systemic by nature. It implies a wide policy focus through integration across often siloed policies, from environmental, regional development, agricultural and industrial ones. Identifying these key sectors and possible synergies is the first step to avoid the implementation of fragmented projects over the short-medium run, due to the lack of a systemic approach.

- **Places**: Cities and regions are not isolated ecosystems, but spaces for inflows and outflows of materials, resources and products, in connection with surrounding areas and beyond. Therefore, adopting a functional approach going beyond the administrative boundaries of cities is important for resource management and economic development. Linkages across urban and rural areas (e.g. related to bio-economy, agriculture and forest) are key to promote local production and recycling of organic residuals to be used in proximity of where they are produced, to avoid negative externalities due to transport. At the regional level, loops related to a series of economic activities (e.g. to the bio-economy) can be closed and slowed.

As a result and in accordance with predefined short-, medium- and long-term objectives, cities and regions can play a role as *promoters*, *facilitators* and *enablers* in the transition from a linear to a circular economy. In practice:

- Cities can **promote** the circular economy as illustrated by the roadmaps and strategies set out in cities like Brussels (Belgium), Paris (France), Amsterdam (Netherlands) and London (United Kingdom). These strategies identified priorities, promoted a number of concrete projects and engaged stakeholders.
- Cities can **facilitate** connections across business, citizens and levels of government. They help direct and facilitate contacts, inform about existing projects, provide soft and hard infrastructure for new circular businesses. The city of Phoenix (United States), for example, created together with the Arizona State University a Resource Innovation and Solutions Network (RISN) Incubator for accompanying businesses in the shift towards a circular economy. In 2017, the city of Paris, France, launched a circular economy incubator, hosting 19 start-ups.
- Cities can **enable** the circular economy transition to happen by providing the appropriate governance and economic tools. Cities can set up incentives, catalyse funds, adapt regulations, etc. For example, the London Waste and Recycling Board (LWARB) in London (United Kingdom) proposed to develop a venture capital fund, seeking private sector partners to join; the city of Amsterdam (Netherlands) created a revolving sustainability fund for businesses to pay back within 15 years with a very low interest rate.

This analytical framework applied to the case of Valladolid, Spain, will identify the main opportunities and challenges (Chapter 2) as well as tailored policy recommendations to promote, facilitate and enable the circular economy (Chapter 3).

People and firms: A circular community-enhancing innovation

In Valladolid, there is an emerging community of circular entrepreneurs that could act as thematic "ambassadors". The circular economy municipal grants in 2017 and 2018 have been an important driver to create a circular economy community in Valladolid. According to this community, made by entrepreneurs, micro and small businesses and civil society, the municipal grant served to stimulate innovation, prototypes and projects, while sharing the risks related to these types of experimental activities. Even if the group is still relatively small in size, it can act as a catalyst of change to spread the message to their fellow citizens and other businesses.

The circular entrepreneurs are developing new business models and practices to stimulate the transition towards a circular economy (see Annex A). For example, by:

- Promoting reuse and recycling of goods and products. Some projects, for example, focus on the recycling of laptops' batteries and extinctors' components or the reuse of electronic material. While reducing waste sent to landfill, the major issue is the lack of a profitable market for these secondary products.
- Connecting actors for the supply and demand of secondary material, through an online platform (app) that aims to connect waste producers (supply side) and companies looking for waste as a resource (demand side), so for them to get in touch and reach an agreement, either as a free transfer or by setting a price.
- Developing a certification for circular economy-related industrial processes. Local businesses' representatives consider that a certificate awarding circular economy activities could stimulate businesses, while informing the administration during the selection process of a public tender. This certification could be complete or partial, considering the different phases of the production (e.g.

eco-design, use of recycled material, etc.). The development of a protocol on the requisites to obtain the circular certification is ongoing.
- Stimulating eco-design. Several projects focus on eco-design: from electrical appliances to a modular design for products' components to be easily reused.

Civil society organisations and consumer associations are also fostering the transition to the circular economy. During 2018 and 2019, the Federation of Neighbourhood Associations of Valladolid (*Federación de Asociaciones Vecinales de Valladolid*) created an online circular observatory to share information on the circular economy and monitor citizens' level of engagement. The organisation also developed an online "monitoring game" to promote reuse, raise awareness on the circular economy and signal the location of second-hand objects (Federation of neighbourhood associations of Valladolid, 2019[27]).

Technical and non-technical knowledge on the circular economy can be built by universities, research centre and technological parks. The University of Valladolid (UVa) and the Technological Agricultural Institute of Castile and León (*Instituto Tecnológico Agrario de Castilla y León*, ITACYL) collaborate on bio-economy research projects, while a project on the circular economy is underway. The UVa and the University of Salamanca work together on solutions for digitalising the agro-food sector's value chain. A metabolism study by the University of Valladolid supported the preparation of the food strategy of the city (Lomas and Carpintero, 2017[28]). The University School of Agricultural Engineering (*Escuela Universitaria de Ingeniería Agrícola*, INEA) created a composting plant to reuse agricultural waste, a bank of seeds, a bank of farm implements and a food bank to be shared among producers and to minimise food waste. The school also contributed to creating a shop located in the centre of Valladolid to promote local zero-km food. Several foundations (e.g. CARTIF, CIDAUT) promote research and pilots on biomass, biotechnology and waste valorisation to reuse materials in the building and automotive sectors. All these activities pave the way for further engagement on the circular economy, both in terms of building knowledge and stimulating collaboration with the public and the private sectors.

The technological clusters and the business sector in Valladolid and in Castile and León can contribute to the transition to a circular economy. The Innovative Business Cluster on Efficient Construction (*Agrupación Empresarial Innovadora para la Construcción Eficiente*, AEICE) gathers more than 100 partners within the construction value chain. The cluster aims to foster innovation and find collaborative solutions amongst their partners and other private and public stakeholders, while promoting circular economy practice amongst its members. In 2017, the AEICE committed to the reuse of construction and demolition waste. The Agency of Innovation and Economic Development supported the AEICE in the development of the "Guide for the use of recycled aggregates" (AEICE, 2018[29]) that provides recommendations to the Valladolid municipality on how to include recycled aggregates in public tenders (e.g. introducing the condition of replacing natural aggregates by artificial ones). The cluster's project "Bio-Economy: A Bio-economy strategy for the food industry of Castile and León" (*BioEconomIA: Estrategia de Bioeconomía para la Industria Alimentaria de Castilla y León*) aims to help its member companies adopt circular economy strategies. This is promoted by the Association of Food Industry in Castile and León (*Asociación de la Industria Alimentaria de Castilla y León*, VITARTIS), which represents 47% of the agro-food regional sector and aims to increase the sectors' productivity with a special focus on bio-economy (VITARTIS, 2019[30]).

The artisan sector can play an important role in the transition from a linear to a circular economy. The sector can be particularly key in reusing and repairing activities that require specific skills, for example in the textile sector. Moreover, as argued by the Regional Centre of Entrepreneurs, which gathers around 1 000 small companies (<10 employees), companies increasingly use recycled materials in their production processes. However, there are several obstacles related to the regulation (e.g. lengthy process to obtain permits) and the price of products and goods that might be not competitive.

The Chamber of Commerce of Valladolid developed capacity building programmes on the circular economy. In 2018, the Chamber of Commerce launched a master course in "Digital transformation and the circular economy". The curriculum included product life cycle analysis, eco-design, circular value chains and data mining (Valladolid Chamber of Commerce, 2019[31]). The aim of the master, beyond building specific skills on the circular economy, was also to increase awareness among professionals. The Chamber of Commerce, together with research partners, is creating consulting models for companies willing to adopt circular economy processes.

Policies: Identifying sectors holding potential for the circular economy

All sectors are concerned in a circular economy, but some have higher potential. Often the circular economy in cities and regions is seen as a synonymous of waste recycling but it is more than that. Cities and regions in their circular economy strategies have identified key sectors that show the greatest potential in terms of economic, social and environmental benefits. These sectors include built environment, food, water, and textile amongst others. According to local specificities, cities and regions are setting up circular economy initiatives for less traditional sectors, such as fashion and culture.

Making a sector "circular" implies rethinking value chains and production and consumption processes. "Circularity" implies that any output can be an input for something else within and across sectors. It aims to: make products and goods last longer through better design; produce goods using secondary and reusable materials, and renewable energy, while reducing atmospheric emissions; produce and distribute products locally and consume them in a conscious and sustainable manner; and transform waste into a resource (Figure 2.3).

Figure 2.3. Circularity within and across sectors

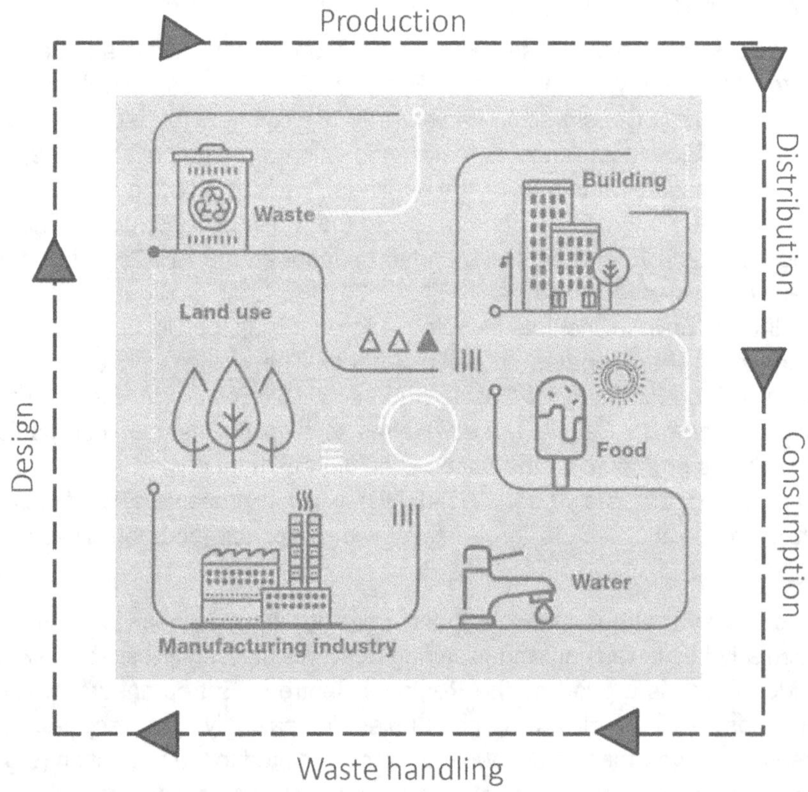

Source: OECD (forthcoming[8]), *The Circular Economy in Cities and Regions*, Synthesis Report, OECD Publishing, Paris.

Various sectors can be taken into account when it comes to fostering the transition from a linear to a circular economy in Valladolid, Spain. According to the results of the *OECD Survey on the Circular Economy in Cities and Regions* (2019[32]), the municipality identified the following sectors as of interest for a circular economy strategy in Valladolid: land use and spatial planning, manufacturing industry, waste, textile, mobility, water, food and beverage, retail, sanitation and construction and demolition (Figure 2.4). Below, specific attention will be dedicated to those sectors that more prominently stand out from the discussion with various stakeholders in Valladolid. This is key to establish the role of the "do-ers" (e.g. entrepreneurs, SMEs, private companies, CSOs, etc.) in the transition from a linear to a circular economy and foresee coherent policies for the future. Information on the sectors included in other cities' and regions' circular economy initiatives is presented in Table 2.5.

Figure 2.4. Sectors of interest for a circular economy strategy in Valladolid, Spain

Source: Own elaboration based on the city of Valladolid's answers to the OECD (2019[32]) OECD Survey on the Circular Economy in Cities and Regions.

The city took the first step to identify the economic sectors that have potential for the circular economy. The city financed a study called "Valladolid is Circular" (Enviroo, 2019[33]), in order to identify the potential of specific economic activities, such as: agriculture, public administration, hospitality industry, education, manufacture of other non-metallic minerals, metallurgy, retail industry, energy supply, real estate activities, food industries and manufacture of motor vehicles, trailers and semi-trailers. The evaluation took into account three factors: value added, job creation and environmental impacts (e.g. water and energy consumption, waste production, etc.). Agriculture is considered the sector with the biggest potential for the circular economy, driven mainly by its environmental impacts. Public administration ranked second mainly because of its importance as the main employer in the city (21 370 employees); followed by the hospitality sector for its value-added contribution to the local economy (6.71% of the total) (Enviroo, 2019[33]). The study concluded with some recommendations, such as:

- Carrying out an innovative public procurement procedure adding social and environmental clauses in tenders.
- Promoting the implementation of environmental management systems in companies through information and training.
- Labelling of products according to the circular economy criteria.
- Favouring waste separation, exploring linkages among sectors and identifying existing barriers to reuse and recycling.
- Promoting the Life Cycle Analysis (LCA) of products and carbon footprint reduction strategies.
- Raising awareness through ad hoc campaigns, for example in schools in Valladolid.

The 61 projects that benefitted from the municipal grants in 2017-18 focus on the following sectors: energy (portable solar kit; use of hydrogen as an alternative fuel); waste (improving the selective waste collection system using real-time data; exchange platform of secondary materials; compost and bio-fertilisers from farming waste; micro-recycling, reducing waste in the catering industry; biodegradable prototype packaging); water (reuse of rainwater in public institutions; network of water dispensers; educative games), and; building (cradle-to-cradle products development) (Annex A).

Table 2.5. Example of sectors included in circular economy initiatives at the subnational level

City/Region	Initiative	Waste	Construction and demolition	Land use and spatial planning	Food and beverage	Manufacturing industry	Textile	Water and sanitation	Energy	Biomass	Agriculture	Mobility	ICT sector	Forestry	Culture
Amsterdam (Netherlands)	Amsterdam Circular 2020-25	✓	✓	✓	✓	✓	✓	✓	✓	✓	✓	✓	✓		
Barcelona Metropolitan Area (AMB) (Spain)	Circular Economy Promotion Programme AMB Circular (2019)		✓	✓	✓			✓	✓	✓	✓	✓			
Flanders (Belgium)	Circular Flanders (2016)	✓	✓	✓	✓	✓		✓					✓		
Greater Porto Area (Portugal)	LIPOR's commitment to circular economy principles (2018)	✓		✓	✓		✓	✓	✓		✓	✓			
Nantes (France)	Circular Economy Roadmap	✓	✓	✓	✓				✓	✓	✓	✓			
North Karelia (Finland)	CIRCWASTE – Towards Circular Economy in North Karelia	✓	✓	✓	✓	✓		✓	✓	✓	✓	✓		✓	
Paris (France)	Circular Economy Plan of Paris 2017-20	✓	✓	✓					✓	✓					✓
Rotterdam (Netherlands)	Rotterdam Circularity Programme 2019-23	✓	✓	✓	✓	✓		✓	✓	✓	✓				
Scotland (United Kingdom)	Circular Glasgow	✓	✓		✓	✓	✓		✓		✓		✓	✓	
Tilburg (Netherlands)	Tilburg Circular Agenda 2019	✓	✓	✓	✓	✓	✓			✓					
Valladolid (Spain)	Valladolid Circular Economy Roadmap (2017-18)		✓	✓	✓	✓	✓	✓		✓		✓		✓	

Source: OECD (forthcoming[8]), *The Circular Economy in Cities and Regions*, Synthesis Report, OECD Publishing, Paris.

Waste

The municipality is responsible for the waste management system in Valladolid. By law,[5] the local government is responsible for providing waste collection and treatment services. The municipality has implemented a selective household waste collection system that collects organic and non-organic waste separately. Regarding non-organic waste streams, the separate collection of paper, glass, batteries and domestic oil is carried out in individual containers. Plastic and metallic packaging are separated in Valladolid's waste treatment centre (*Centro de Tratamiento de Residuos de Valladolid*, CTR) where all collected waste is treated. Different companies, registered under the Integrated Management System, provide waste containers and waste collection vehicles. This is the case of ECOVIDRIO for glass and Ecoembes for paper, carton, plastic and metallic packaging (Box 2.4). The municipality has also created five "clean spots" (*Puntos limpios*) where households can deploy toxic or voluminous residues. Valladolid is one of the three municipalities in Spain that finances the waste management system through the general taxation system (Fundació ENT Catalunya, 2018[34]). In 2015, the local government removed the waste tax[6] that had been in place from 2013 to 2015. This tax used to collect EUR 10 million per year (Valladolid Municipality, 2015[35]).

The Business Confederation of Valladolid (*Confederación Vallisoletana de Empresarios*, CVE) runs a pilot project to reduce waste management costs by fostering separate collection. Information related to the quantity and quality of waste produced by the companies participating in the project was shared with the waste department of the municipality of Valladolid in order to re-organise the waste collection system in a more efficient way by using real-time data and to put in place a penalty system in case of misbehaviour. Other circular economy initiatives related to the waste sector are detailed in Annex A. One example is the platform for the exchange of secondary materials developed by the Valladolid Business and Professionals Association (*Asociación de empresas y profesionales*, EDUCA).

Box 2.4. Circular economy initiatives by the Ecoembes

Ecoembes is a non-profit environmental organisation responsible throughout Spain for promoting and managing the system for recycling household packaging waste. Ecoembes gathers more than 12 000 companies that by law (*Ley 11/1997 de 24 de abril, de Envases y Residuos de Envases,* Law on Packaging and Packaging Waste)[7] are requested to finance a system of selective collection and recycling of household packaging.

Ecoembes promotes the circular economy through several initiatives in Spain:

- **The CircularLab**: The lab promotes collaboration with companies, public administrations and citizens of the Autonomous Community of La Rioja (Spain) to develop best practices in all phases of the packaging life cycle, from eco-design to its reintroduction to the consumption cycle through new products.
- **La Victoria neighbourhood**: In 2018, the City Council of Valladolid and Ecoembes started a pilot project of the circular economy in the neighbourhood of La Victoria. The objective of the project is to achieve separate collection by 60% by 2030, in line with the European objectives. The initiative began in March 2018 and concluded in April 2019. The percentage of waste disposed of for selective collection rose from 32.8% of the total in March, when the campaign began, to 51.3% in April 2019.
- **Recycling 5.0 project**: Launched in 2019, the project aims to encourage recycling through an application that allows citizens to connect their mobile phones to the containers. The user will take a picture of the bar code of each bottle deposited in the yellow bin and link the action with the QR code present in the container. The system digitally registers all the activities and,

> depending on the amount of bottles recycled, it provides users with credits to be exchanged products or services that contribute to achieve sustainability goals. Four municipalities, two universities and a hospital in Catalonia are piloting the project.
> - **Sterling project**: It consists of the installation of ten intelligent yellow containers for plastic containers and cans on the Valladolid Campus. These containers are equipped with filling, temperature and humidity sensors. Through an app, the containers are able to automatically identify the users who use them. Each time the Sterling container is used, the user will receive a Sterling point. Each month, participants who have accumulated ten or more Sterling points can win one of the three gift cards (equivalent to EUR 20) offered by the project organisers. The project benefitted from municipal grants launched in 2018.
>
> Source: Ecoembes (2019[36]), *Homepage*, https://www.ecoembes.com/es (accessed on 7 June 2019); The Circular Lab (2019[37]), The Circular Lab (2019), *Homepage*, http://www.thecircularlab.com (accessed on 7 June 2019); European Circular Economy Stakeholder Platform (2018[38]), *Citizen Participation and Circular Economy: A Pilot Project in the City Hall of Valladolid*, https://circulareconomy.europa.eu/platform/en/good-practices/citizen-participation-and-circular-economy-pilot-project-city-hall-valladolid (accessed on 7 June 2019); Valladolid Municipality (2018[39]), "El Ayuntamiento y Ecoembes impulsan un proyecto piloto de economía circular para lograr el correcto depósito del 60% de los residuos en un año", http://www.valladolid.es/es/actualidad/noticias/ayuntamiento-ecoembes-impulsan-proyecto-piloto-economia-cir (accessed on 7 June 2019); University of Valladolid Website (2019[40]), *Homepage*, http://comunicacion.uva.es/export/sites/comunicacion/98240de9-350c-11e9-b081-d59857eb090a/ (accessed on 7 June 2019).

Valladolid has been a pioneer in introducing organic waste separation in the metropolitan area. Organic waste collection, the responsibility of the municipality, started two decades ago in Valladolid and a facility upgrade has been planned. After the collection process, the organic waste is treated, producing compost and stabilised bio-waste. The compost produced is used in the rural areas located in the surroundings of the composting plant, predominantly to grow cereal. This compost is of low quality and cannot be certified in ecological terms.[8] As such, it can be reclaimed for free by local producers. A tender for constructing a modern composting plant is under preparation. The new plant will increase the quality of the compost and make it profitable. It will be located in the outskirts of Valladolid and should be operative by 2020. So far, there is no waste resources plan to define clear goals and vision although a draft plan has been elaborated aiming to move up the waste hierarchy following the EU approach (Box 2.5). The draft plan is expected to be approved by July 2020.

> ### Box 2.5. The EU's approach to waste management
>
> In the last 30 years, the European Union (EU) waste policy has aimed to reduce negative environmental and health impacts through the creation of an energy and resource-efficient economy and to limit the amount of waste generation associated with economic growth.
>
> The Waste Framework Directive is the cornerstone of EU waste policy. The directive established a five-step waste hierarchy. Waste prevention and reduction is the top priority, followed by reuse, recycling and other forms of recovery, with disposal (e.g. landfill) as the last resort. EU waste legislation aims to move waste management up the waste hierarchy (Figure 2.5).
> - **Prevention**: Successful waste management is able to prevent waste generation in the first place. Waste prevention and reduction are increasingly important as the global population and demand for finite natural resources increases.
> - **Reuse**: Consists of the repeated use of products or its components for the same purpose for which they were designed (e.g. refrigerators, ink cartridges).

- **Recycling**: Reduces the amount of waste that ends up in landfill sites while cutting down on the amount of material needed from the natural environment. In 2016, Spain only recycled 29.7% of its municipal waste and this level stayed almost the same since 2010.
- **Energy recovery**: Energy recovery reduces carbon emissions by replacing the use of fossil-fuel-based energy sources and substituting methane emissions generated in landfills. It is usually applied to different methods for converting waste into energy (e.g. electricity, steam and heating for buildings). However, energy recovery through incineration is often not the most efficient way of managing used materials. Life cycle analysis is encouraged to identify the net environmental benefits and damages of waste incineration. A total of 13% of municipal waste in Spain is used for energy recovery.
- **Disposal**: Landfill is the least desirable option due to its numerous negative environmental impacts. The most severe is the production and release of methane into the air (25 times more potent than carbon dioxide). If converted to energy, the methane produced by an average municipal landfill could provide electricity to approximately 20 000 households for a year. In Spain, 56.7% of municipal waste was sent to landfill in 2016 (EAE, 2018[41]).

Figure 2.5. Waste hierarchy in the EU

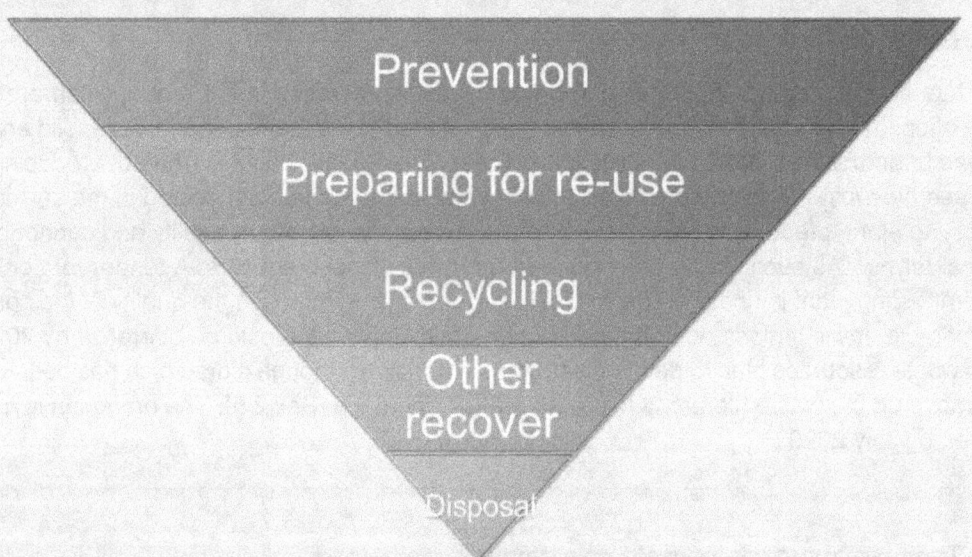

Source: EC (2010[42]), *Being Wise with Waste: The EU's Approach to Waste Management*, https://ec.europa.eu/environment/waste/pdf/WASTE%20BROCHURE.pdf (accessed on 29 November 2019).

In December 2015, the European Commission (EC) adopted a package to support the EU's transition to a circular economy. The initiative was designed to contribute to "closing the loop" of product lifecycles through greater recycling and reuse and bring benefits for both the environment and the economy. Additional measures and updates followed in 2018 and 2019. The package included the EU Action Plan for the Circular Economy outlining 54 measures addressing various aspects of the circular economy and focusing on 5 priority areas (plastics, food waste, critical raw materials, construction and demolition, and biomass and bio-based products) as well as 4 legislative proposals amending the following legal acts: Waste Framework Directive; Landfill Directive; Packaging Waste Directive; Directives on end-of-life vehicles, on batteries and accumulators and waste batteries and accumulators, and on waste electrical and electronic equipment.

Source: EC (2010[42]), *Being Wise with Waste: The EU's Approach to Waste Management*, https://ec.europa.eu/environment/waste/pdf/WASTE%20BROCHURE.pdf (accessed on 29 November 2019); EC (2008[43]), *Directive 2008/98/EC on Waste (Waste Framework Directive) - Environment*, https://ec.europa.eu/environment/waste/framework/ (accessed on 3 December 2019); EC (2015[44]), *Closing the Loop - An EU Action Plan for the Circular Economy*, https://eur-lex.europa.eu/resource.html?uri=cellar:8a8ef5e8-99a0-11e5-b3b7-01aa75ed71a1.0012.02/DOC_1&format=PDF (accessed on 5 February 2020); EAE (2018[41]), *Gestión de residuos y Economía Circular*, http://marketing.eae.es/prensa/SRC_Residuos.pdf (accessed on 3 December 2019); OECD (forthcoming[8]), *The Circular Economy in Cities and Regions*, Synthesis Report, OECD Publishing, Paris.

Mobility

The municipality of Valladolid is promoting sustainable mobility. As a "lighthouse city",[9] the municipality is part of the European funded project REMOURBAN that aims to foster sustainability and improve citizens' quality of life through energy efficiency, electric mobility and digital technology. As such, it aims at increasing low carbon mobility solutions by 5% in the short term and 25% in the medium term. This change should reduce CO2 emissions by half. The municipality is heading towards an electric public transport fleet, while also offering incentives to companies to use electric vehicles (e.g. to perform last-mile services, conform their business fleets or providing taxi services). The circular economy can stimulate the debate on sustainable mobility (green public transport, electric cars), reuse and dismantling of batteries and rechargers for green mobility and the interaction between land use and mobility to favour a more efficient use of the public space (e.g. car parking, green areas). For example, the city of Paris has planned to develop a local urban planning scheme that aims to preserve existing logistics facilities and to create 15 "urban logistics spaces" (*Espaces Logistiques Urbains, ELU*) to improve logistics and foster shared mobility services (Paris Municipality, 2017[45]).

Building sector

The European and national regulations are advancing towards a more sustainable building sector. The updated EU Energy performance of buildings directive (EPBD) (2018/844/EU), adopted in July 2018, establishes that by 2050 all national building stocks have to be zero-energy buildings. This means that the total amount of energy used by the building on an annual basis is equal to the amount of renewable energy created on the site (EC, 2018[46]). Countries will need to develop a National Energy and Climate Plan (NECP) that defines long-term renovation strategies. Indicative milestones for 2030 and 2040 have been established to assess and monitor progress. At the same time, the directive states that from 2021 all new buildings in the EU must be nearly zero-energy buildings (NZEB). Currently, EU countries need to perform energy-efficient renovations to at least 3% of the total floor area of the buildings owned and used by the central government (EC, 2018[46]).

In Valladolid, initiatives are in place to improve the energy performance of buildings and experiment with new schemes of district heating. Following the EU Energy Efficiency Directive (2012/27/EU), since 2014, the city has committed to make energy efficiency renovations in at least 3% of the city-owned buildings. The municipality set as a priority to maximise the energy efficiency of the public building stock, minimise under-utilised public buildings and generate energy consumption information in order to optimise the use in each building. As part of the EU project REMOURBAN, the municipality advanced in the energy rehabilitation of the 398 homes, with 1 000 inhabitants in a 24 000 m2 area. District heating and hot water are provided by biomass, while electricity is provided by photovoltaic panels installed in the facades of the buildings (Valladolid Municipality, 2017[47]). In some public buildings, such as the Regional Council and on the University of Valladolid campus, biomass is used for heat and hot water. In addition, the Circular Eco-design Centre has been launched in 2019 as a space for collaboration and co-creation of eco-design innovation applied to the habitat and construction value chain (AEICE, 2019[48]).[10] More information on existing circular economy initiatives in the building sector can be found in Annex A.

Water

Promoting drinking water, water reuse and raising awareness on the value of water can be part of a circular economy approach. In Valladolid, actions are carried out to: promote a plastic-free water culture; reuse water for irrigation in public institutions; and use green infrastructure. The reduction of single-use plastic is promoted through the creation of a network of water dispensers in Valladolid and an online map to share their location. Water reuse is fostered through the development of a rainwater collection system in public institutions such as schools. The aim is twofold: reducing the risk for flooding and reusing rainwater to irrigate schools and urban gardens. A third aspect promoted in the sector is raising awareness among students (from school to university) on green infrastructure and the importance of the water cycle in Valladolid.

Hospitality sector

The hospitality sector shows high potential for applying the circular economy approach. The study "Valladolid Circular" (Enviroo, 2019[33]) identified challenges and opportunities for the sector within the circular economy. One of the most prominent issues is the production of waste. As such, the sector is responsible for 70% of organic waste or mixed waste. There is room for improvement in terms of separate collection and energy efficiency. As such, several initiatives are already in place in hotels, restaurants and bars, in order to: i) reduce single plastic use and food waste; ii) create a new business model to recover and transform organic waste collected from bars and restaurants in the city, through waste treatment, and; iii) apply the product-as-a-service business model to the sector offering rental of equipment and machinery for the hotel/restaurant sector. The hospitality sector is likely to generate value added and job creation. Specific circular projects related to the hospitality sector are listed in Annex A.

Places: Fostering urban-rural synergies for the circular economy

The regional bio-economy and the municipal food strategies hold potential in fostering urban-rural synergies. The Municipal Food Strategy (Alimenta Valladolid, 2018[49]) intends to improve the co-ordination between urban and rural areas and create employment opportunities whereby the city can act as an agro-incubator for responsible consumption and local production. It foresees the creation of a "land bank" (*banco de tierras*) that the municipality could rent to local producers at affordable costs. The eco-markets located in the city and its surroundings (e.g. the ecological market located at the Centre of Environmental Resources, *Centro de Recursos Ambientales*, PRAE) are a first step to bring local production to city customers. Moreover, the municipality is planning actions to improve the measurement, tradability and quality of organic waste from urban (e.g. hotel and restaurant sector) and rural areas. The Castile and León's Bio-Economy Strategy (Government of Castile and León, 2019[50]) is the first regional bio-economy strategy in Spain. One of the objectives is to promote the demand and development of markets related to the bio-economy. This can affect the city of Valladolid. Further details on the Castile and León's Bio-Economy Strategy and the Municipal Food Strategy are provided in Box 2.6.

> **Box 2.6. The Castile and León's Bio-Economy Strategy and the Municipal Food Strategy**
>
> The Castile and León's Bio-Economy Strategy (*Programa de Bio-Economía Circular de Castilla y León*) foresees four main lines of action:
>
> 1. Foster public-private research and technological development.
> 2. Raise awareness on the bio-economy.
> 3. Develop a regional supply of bio-economy products and services.
> 4. Promote the demand and development of markets related to bio-economy.
>
> The Food Strategy of Valladolid (*Estrategia Alimentaria de Valladolid*) defines 6 areas of action, covering 13 measures and setting out a total of 66 actions to be implemented in the period 2019-23:
>
> 1. Protection and revitalisation of the productive potential of Valladolid's agricultural land.
> 2. Access to healthy, ecological, diverse and quality food.
> 3. Promotion of local distribution networks.
> 4. Culture of responsible food.
> 5. Food waste prevention.
> 6. Good governance and inter- and intra-administrative co-ordination.
>
> The strategy aims to create a municipal food council formed by the local sectoral actors (public, private and civil society organisations) that have been contributing to the strategy since 2017. The future municipal food council will be responsible for monitoring the implementation of the strategy's goals. The strategy will map the relevant stakeholders that take part in the local agro-food sector and the existing economic and social networks among them to foster potential synergies throughout the sector's value chain.
>
> Source: Alimenta Valladolid (2018[49]), *Valladolid's Food Strategy*, http://www.alimentavalladolid.info/ (accessed on 11 June 2019); Government of Castile and León (2019[50]), *Castile and Leon's Bio-economy Strategy*, http://www.redei.es/images/2018/Estrategia_ICE_Bioeconom%C3%ADa.pdf (accessed on 11 June 2019); ITACYL (2019[51]), *Plan de Impulso a la Bioeonomía Agroalimentaria para un Entorno Rural Competitivo y Sostenible en Castilla y León*, http://www.itacyl.es/documents/20143/0/PlanImpulsoBioeconomiaAgroalimentaria_2019.pdf/34554980-e0c5-bcca-6420-b5c8ec857cd8 (accessed on 18 October 2019).

There are several examples of circular related activities in the agriculture sector in Valladolid and its surroundings. Some good practices from companies located in the surroundings of Valladolid have been identified in the agro-food and livestock sector. Practices consist in: reducing food waste and water consumption during the processing and packaging phases; donating food with visual defects to food banks and making it available to vulnerable families; reusing organic waste; reducing the use of chemical additives (INEA, 2018[52]). Other practices that can be linked to a circular economy approach consist in promoting urban agriculture.

Metropolitan co-operation holds the potential to further strengthen service provision in a sustainable and circular way. The Association of General Urban Interest, former Urban Community of Valladolid (*Comunidad Urbana de Valladolid*, CUVA) aims to provide services in a co-ordinated manner to the almost 410 000 inhabitants living in the metropolitan area of Valladolid. The 25 member municipalities are working together to better connect each other through public transportation, sharing wastewater treatment facilities, and in the implementation of the food strategy. At the metropolitan level, the circular economy can be fostered by identifying resource streams in the area, creating a community of practice and using public procurement to stimulate circular products, amongst others.

Governance challenges to design and implement the circular transition

Mostly, the challenges cities and regions are facing in building circular economies are not of a technical but of an economic and governance nature. Technical solutions exist and are well known. However, to implement them, information and financial resources are needed, as well as an updated legal frameworks. Often, a holistic vision is still missing because of siloed policies. Cultural barriers are still a very important obstacle (OECD, forthcoming[8]). Key governance challenges to design and implement the circular transition in Valladolid, Spain, are presented below.

The development and implementation of the circular economy strategy will demand more effective co-ordination among municipal departments and a clearer definition of the allocation of roles and responsibilities. There are no institutional incentives for horizontal co-ordination at the technical level, nor specific co-ordination mechanisms or joint programmes amongst municipal departments. This can generate duplications and costs inefficiencies. For example, municipal departments agree that the design of bicycle lanes was a missed opportunity for collaboration across: urbanism, infrastructure and housing; citizen participation, youth and sports, and environment and sustainability departments. Further co-ordination will be needed across municipal departments in charge of environment, mobility, social and economic activities, in order to maximise synergies and investments for the circular economy.

Co-ordination across levels of government is needed to align the goals of national, regional and local circular economy strategies, as well as to adapt the regulatory (e.g. green regulation) and fiscal system (e.g. preventing double VAT charges for secondary material) to the transition to a circular economy. Some examples of coordination are the following: the National Co-ordination Waste Commission involves national, regional and local authorities, represented by the FEMP. This commission integrates 12 technical working groups (one per waste stream), including a specific one on the circular economy. There is also an Inter-ministerial Committee for the Circular Economy.

The issue of scale is key for the circular economy to take place and to move from experimentation to business as usual. In the case of Valladolid, a total of 61 projects benefitted from municipal grants for the circular economy in 2017-18. Projects are related to different sectors and type of activities: from awareness-raising to knowledge building or technological development. Nevertheless, they are mostly carried out at the neighbourhood or individual scale. In order to achieve the expected social, economic and environmental impacts of the circular economy, these projects should be scaled up after the experimentation phase.

Policy coherence should be fostered and existing circular economy-related initiatives could benefit from greater coherence and a long-term view. Policy coherence is linked with the long-term vision of the city. Three main challenges can be identified:

- *Coherence across existing policies and plans*: Valladolid is implementing different policies and programmes (e.g. Smart City Programme, urban sustainable mobility, green infrastructure, district heating, circular economy) that would benefit from a more holist approach and from greater co-ordination to close loops. Currently, it is not clear how the abovementioned policies connect to one another in a coherent manner. For example, the New General Urban Plan (2019) that promotes a compact city model could be linked to various actions in complementary sectors that foster circularity in the city, from mobility to infrastructure.
- *Coherence across current and future circular projects*: At the moment, there is the risk of delivering isolated circular economy actions while missing the long-term vision. It is unclear how the selected projects will contribute to the overall vision of the city of Valladolid.
- *Coherence across EU funded projects and circular economy-planned initiatives*: The city relies heavily on European funds for policy innovation. However, initiatives can result in fragmented actions, which could be oriented short- to medium-term. The municipality conceives the European projects as a way of experimenting with new policies without using local taxpayers' money and as

an opportunity to foster public-private partnerships under the "consortium agreement" model. For example, the mentioned REMOURBAN project that focused on improving buildings' energy efficiency was applied to the residential FASA district, a neighbour located in the South-East of the city, but was not integrated into a city-level strategy. The same happened with the biomass district heating system installed by the municipality in the FASA neighbourhood that was not part of a broader plan. The municipality would need to clarify how to maximise synergies between these initiatives and those planned within the circular economy approach.

Capacities in the municipality should be built to match the needs of the circular economy transition, in terms of skills and human resources. Adapting the responsible authorities' capacity level to the complexity of the circular economy challenges is key. The Agency of Innovation and Economic Development in charge of the development of the Circular Economy Strategy, as well as of the implementation of several EU-funded projects on sustainability, mobility and energy efficiency is composed of a group of 17 motivated and competent people. It is expected that more staff would be needed to meet the workload on the circular economy (e.g. to support business, organise events, etc.). Similarly, given the multi-disciplinary nature of the circular economy, the municipality should evaluate whether the needs of the circular economy transition match the skills and human resources available within the municipality departments.

Efforts to improve the environmental, social and economic database are ongoing but there is room for improvement in terms of data availability and frequency. Data sources are fragmented across different agencies, e.g. the Urban Observatory (*Valladolid en cifras*), the "Air pollution control network of the city of Valladolid" (*Red de Control de Contaminación Atmosférica del Ayuntamiento de Valladolid*, RCCAVA), the waste treatment centre (*Centro de Tratamiento de Residuos de Valladolid*, CTR Valladolid), the housing institute (*Sociedad Municipal de Suelo y Vivienda*, VIVA), the environmental control section (*Sección de control ambiental*), the public bus company (*Autobuses Urbanos de Valladolid S.A.*, AUVASA), and the water management company (*Agua de Valladolid E.P.E.*, Aquavall). Data referring to the waste and energy sectors, which are key for the circular economy, are not publicly available or presented in a systematic way. The municipal information system (e.g. *Valladolid en Cifras*) does not provide updated public data on air pollution; waste production and recycling; water consumption and reuse; or flooding risks.

Information on the circular economy should be improved. There is a lack of understanding of the potential benefits of the circular economy and scarce interest from companies and citizens. More than 70% of companies in Valladolid of a total of 70 companies surveyed in 2018 declared that they do not know the meaning of the circular economy. They associate the term to minimising waste production, recycling and reusing and they state that they are already implementing these processes in a regular way (EDUCA, 2018[53]). On the other hand, 85% of consumers in Valladolid do not know what the circular economy means and only 52% of consumers expressed they "always" or "regularly" separate waste (EDUCA, 2018[53]). Citizens tend to feel no obligation to separate waste because they are already paying taxes for that (not linked to their waste generation). While separated collection is compulsory, there is no enforcement on waste collection. The lack of waste separation generates extra costs for the municipality at the collection and treatment steps.

Public funds to start and scale-up projects in relation to a circular economy are limited and access to other sources is not easy. The municipality subsidised 61 projects in 2017-18. Most of the projects related to the circular economy (whether concerning a new design for more durable products, use of secondary material in production processes or transformation of waste into resources) still have an experimental nature. Their profitability is uncertain. Entrepreneurs face a high investment risks and maintenance costs (e.g. the costs of secondary materials compared to virgin ones). This situation adds to the fact that access to loans is not always guaranteed. As such, innovators rely on business angels willing to promote and finance circular economy projects, ethical banking (Fiare,[11] Triodos),[12] financial agencies (Finnova)[13] or private equity firms. After this initial phase, the challenge for innovators is how to make their projects economically sustainable in the medium and long terms.

Valladolid, like other municipalities, needs to consider how fiscal and economic tools could incentivise the transition towards a circular economy. A range of economic and fiscal instruments can be used to shift behaviour towards greater environmental responsibility for citizens and business (Box 2.7). Local taxes (e.g. the waste tax) or specific incentives (e.g. discounts) can incentivise behaviour with regards to increasing separate collection. However, criteria for defining the level of taxation should be clear as well as the incentive for the citizens. This requires also enforcement measures. In Valladolid, a waste tax was introduced between 2012 and 2015 and then removed for political reasons.

Box 2.7. Examples of economic instruments for the circular economy

Economic instruments are tools for incentivising or disincentivising specific behaviours. For example, they could induce, by means of higher/lower prices, more sustainable consumption; value-added tax (VAT) exemptions can help businesses use green technologies; incentives on renewable energy can support its wider use. According to the European Energy Agency (2016), to date, efforts have been fundamentally focused on the area of energy, transport and climate, with limited action in relation to issues of pollution and resource use. However, there are several examples:

- **Discounts on taxes**: in 2018, the city of Milan (Italy) developed actions to address food waste, including a 20% discount on waste tax for businesses (supermarkets, restaurants, canteens, producers, etc.) that donated their food waste to charities. The action is co-ordinated by different municipality departments (fiscal, environmental, food policy). Around 10 000 businesses have benefitted from this tax reduction, with an impact of EUR 1.8 million. The city of Shanghai (China) has offered VAT reductions to a recycling company working on the circular economy project of the city. The city of San Francisco granted discounts on their waste fees to businesses using separate sorting collection bins, which allowed San Francisco to become the city in the United States with the least amount of waste going to landfills. With the aim of stimulating the separate disposal of food waste, the city of San Sebastian (Spain) provided households with a specific organic waste collector located in the street and unlockable using a personal magnetic card. The use of this special bin is associated with a 15% reduction on the waste collection service fee. In order to get the discount, users must use this container at least 4 times a month for 10 of the 12 months of the year.

- **Differentiated tariffs**: The Dutch Government implemented the DIFTAR system, a recollecting scheme based on differentiated tariffs in order to provide incentives to improve waste separation at source. This scheme enables authorities to charge for the generated amount of waste, while it rewards the effort of people who minimise waste and maximise separate collection. The system has been introduced in several small towns in the Netherlands as well as in some urban municipalities with over 100 000 inhabitants such as Apeldoorn, Nijmegen and Maastricht.

Source: Food and Agriculture Organization of the United Nations (2018[54]), *Milan: A Comprehensive Food Policy to Tackle Food Waste*, http://www.fao.org/3/ca0901en/CA0901EN.pdf (accessed on 7 June 2019); OECD (2013[55]), *Scaling-up Finance Mechanisms for Biodiversity*, https://dx.doi.org/10.1787/9789264193833-en; European Parliamentary Research Service (2017[56]), *Towards a Circular Economy – Waste Management in the EU STUDY Science and Technology Options Assessment*, http://www.europarl.europa.eu/RegData/etudes/STUD/2017/581913/EPRS_STU%282017%29581913_EN.pdf (accessed on 5 June 2019); San Sebastian City Council (2016[57]), San Sebastian City Council (2016), "Aprobada la bonificación del 15% en la tasa de basura por utilizar el quinto contenedor", http://www.donostia.eus/home.nsf/0/DD2431ECEA04493EC1257F4D004D1232 (accessed on 5 June 2019); CNBC (2018[58]), "San Francisco leads the world when it comes to waste management", http://www.cnbc.com/2018/07/13/how-san-francisco-became-a-global-leader-in-waste-management.html (accessed on 7 June 2019); OECD (forthcoming[8]), *The Circular Economy in Cities and Regions*, Synthesis Report, OECD Publishing, Paris.

The regulatory framework can be improved to allow circularity. Regulation for preventing food waste or towards clearer criteria to use waste as a resource have a supranational or national connotation. In Spain, there is a Food Waste Strategy and a Food Waste Panel for an early evaluation of food waste. Nevertheless, there is a discussion of a food waste methodology at the EU level, which will be incorporated in the national strategy. At the same time, according to waste regulations, Spanish authorities are making progress in evaluating organic by-products in order to reduce food waste and improve circularity.

Although environmental criteria have been added in public procurement, in practice, price is still the prevailing awarding criterion. The city has approved Municipal Ordinance 1/2018 to Promote Social Efficient Procurement: Strategic, exhaustive and sustainable. The ordinance includes environmental dimensions, entailing that the subject and pricing of municipal contracts should consider life cycle criteria or the most innovative, efficient and sustainable solutions. Expected impacts are related to reducing air pollution, using recycled material and promoting recycling. The municipality has incorporated environmental standards into the tenders to offer public land or old buildings for private investment. In the assessment of contracts, the awarding criteria make explicit references to the circular economy, in terms of use of raw materials, sustainable products, life cycle analysis, useful life, energy efficiency, less maintenance and more sustainable packaging. Nonetheless, the final decision is 60% driven by price and 40% driven by an "improvement criterion" (of which 20% is related to social aspects). Moreover, when introducing environmental criteria, there is the risk for tenders going empty or for companies complaining about the possible threat of anti-rivalry clauses, claiming that only big companies can meet some specific requirements. Finally, there are also difficulties in verifying the information provided by the participants to the tenders, when it comes to environmental dimensions.

Innovation in the business sector is key in the circular economy. However, there is a lack of start-ups in Valladolid that could contribute to this innovation. The economy of Valladolid is mainly characterised by the tertiary sector with little innovation capacity; agro-companies are located elsewhere in the region, while big automotive companies located in Valladolid have their headquarters abroad. As such, the latter do not take the lead in implementing circular changes in business models. The weak link with universities and research centres and the lack of incubators, jointly with endogenous social characteristics (e.g. ageing population), do not create a fertile environment for innovation.

Stakeholder engagement is still not fully exploited. Through the EU-funded projects and the Circular Weekend mentioned above, the city of Valladolid has been working towards greater stakeholder engagement, especially in terms of fostering information and participation. However, there is still room to further improve levels of stakeholder engagement and collaboration. For example, there is no real collaboration across public, private and academic actors. The local government could enhance collaboration with universities and companies in the area, and make the city available as a test-bed for technical and non-technical innovation.

References

AEICE (2019), *Visión de AEICE sobre el papel del sector del hábitat en la transformación hacia la economía circular*. [48]

AEICE (2018), *Guía para la utilización de árido reciclado y recomendaciones para su compra*, https://www.aeice.org/wp-content/uploads/2018/11/Guia_ECOCIVIL.pdf (accessed on 25 October 2019). [29]

Agency of Innovation and Economic Development (2019), *Objetivos programáticos y líneas básicas de la acción de gobierno 2019-2023*, Valladolid City Council, Valladolid, http://www.valladolidadelante.es (accessed on 6 June 2019). [14]

Alimenta Valladolid (2018), *Valladolid's Food Strategy*, http://www.alimentavalladolid.info/ (accessed on 11 June 2019). [49]

C40 Cities (2016), *C40 Good Practice Guides: Amsterdam - Sustainability Fund and Amsterdam Climate and Energy Fund*, http://www.c40.org/case_studies/c40-good-practice-guides-amsterdam-sustainability-fund-and-amsterdam-climate-energy-fund (accessed on 6 June 2019). [15]

Castile and León Environment Department (2018), *Jornadas Economía Circular 2017-2018*, https://medioambiente.jcyl.es/web/jcyl/MedioAmbiente/es/Plantilla100Detalle/1246988359553/_/1284752296638/Comunicacion?plantillaObligatoria=PlantillaContenidoNoticiaHome (accessed on 31 May 2019). [12]

CNBC (2018), "San Francisco leads the world when it comes to waste management", http://www.cnbc.com/2018/07/13/how-san-francisco-became-a-global-leader-in-waste-management.html (accessed on 7 June 2019). [58]

EAE (2018), *Gestión de residuos y Economía Circular*, http://marketing.eae.es/prensa/SRC_Residuos.pdf (accessed on 3 December 2019). [41]

EC (2019), *Improving Access to Finance for Circular Economy Projects*, European Commission, http://dx.doi.org/10.2777/983129. [17]

EC (2018), *Energy Performance of Buildings Directive*, European Commission, https://ec.europa.eu/energy/en/topics/energy-efficiency/energy-performance-of-buildings/energy-performance-buildings-directive (accessed on 2 December 2019). [46]

EC (2015), *Closing the Loop - An EU Action Plan for the Circular Economy*, COM/2015/0614, European Commission, https://eur-lex.europa.eu/resource.html?uri=cellar:8a8ef5e8-99a0-11e5-b3b7-01aa75ed71a1.0012.02/DOC_1&format=PDF (accessed on 5 February 2020). [44]

EC (2010), *Being Wise with Waste: The EU's Approach to Waste Management*, European Commission, https://ec.europa.eu/environment/waste/pdf/WASTE%20BROCHURE.pdf (accessed on 29 November 2019). [42]

EC (2008), *Directive 2008/98/EC on Waste (Waste Framework Directive) - Environment*, European Commission, https://ec.europa.eu/environment/waste/framework/ (accessed on 3 December 2019). [43]

Ecoembes (2019), *Homepage*, https://www.ecoembes.com/es (accessed on 7 June 2019). [36]

EDUCA (2018), *Asociación de Empresas y Profesionales EDUCA*, https://www.educavalladolid.es/ (accessed on 2 February 2020). [53]

EIB (2019), *The EIB Circular Economy Guide: Supporting the Circular Transition*, European Investment Bank, http://www.eib.org/attachments/thematic/circular_economy_guide_en.pdf (accessed on 2 August 2019). [18]

Enviroo (2019), *Valladolid EScircular*, http://www.escircular.com (accessed on 11 June 2019). [33]

European Circular Economy Stakeholder Platform (2018), *Citizen Participation and Circular Economy: A Pilot Project in the City Hall of Valladolid*, https://circulareconomy.europa.eu/platform/en/good-practices/citizen-participation-and-circular-economy-pilot-project-city-hall-valladolid (accessed on 7 June 2019). [38]

European Parliamentary Research Service (2017), *Towards a Circular Economy - Waste Management in the EU STUDY Science and Technology Options Assessment*, http://www.europarl.europa.eu/RegData/etudes/STUD/2017/581913/EPRS_STU%282017%299581913_EN.pdf (accessed on 5 June 2019). [56]

Federation of neighbourhood associations of Valladolid (2019), *Actividades de economía circular de la federación*. [27]

FEMP (2019), *La Estrategia Local de economía circular*, Federación Española de Municipios y Provincias, http://www.femp.es/comunicacion/noticias/la-estrategia-local-de-economia-circular (accessed on 21 October 2019). [6]

Food and Agriculture Organization of the United Nations (2018), *Milan: A Comprehensive Food Policy to Tackle Food Waste*, Food and Agriculture Organization of the United Nations, http://www.fao.org/3/ca0901en/CA0901EN.pdf (accessed on 7 June 2019). [54]

Fundació ENT Catalunya (2018), *Las tasas de residuos en España 2018*, https://www.fiscalitatresidus.org/wp-content/uploads/2019/01/Estudio-tasas_2018.pdf (accessed on 29 November 2019). [34]

Government of Castile and León (2019), *Castile and Leon's Bio-economy Strategy*, http://www.redei.es/images/2018/Estrategia_ICE_Bioeconom%C3%ADa.pdf (accessed on 11 June 2019). [50]

Government of Spain (2020), *ACUERDO DE CONSEJO DE MINISTROS POR EL QUE SE APRUEBA LA DECLARACIÓN DEL GOBIERNO ANTE LA EMERGENCIA CLIMÁTICA Y AMBIENTAL*, https://www.miteco.gob.es/es/prensa/declaracionemergenciaclimatica_tcm30-506551.pdf (accessed on 26 February 2020). [3]

Government of Spain (2018), *España Circular 2030, Estrategia Española de Economía Circular*, Gobierno de España, http://www.miteco.gob.es/images/es/180206economiacircular_tcm30-440922.pdf (accessed on 31 May 2019). [1]

INE (2020), *Número de municipios por provincias, comunidades autónomas e islas*. [7]

INEA (2018), *Buenas Prácticas en Empresas Agroalimentarias*, http://www.inea.org (accessed on 11 June 2019). [52]

ITACYL (2019), *Plan de Impulso a la Bioeonomía Agroalimentaria para un Entorno Rural Competitivo y Sostenible en Castilla y León*, http://www.itacyl.es/documents/20143/0/PlanImpulsoBioeconomiaAgroalimentaria_2019.pdf/34554980-e0c5-bcca-6420-b5c8ec857cd8 (accessed on 18 October 2019). [51]

Lomas, P. and O. Carpintero (2017), *Metabolismo y Huella ecológicade la alimentación: El caso de Valladolid (Diagnóstico para la Estrategia Alimentaria Local)*, http://www.alimentavalladolid.info/wp-content/uploads/2017/11/Metabolismo-Alimentario-Valladolid_definitivo.pdf (accessed on 21 October 2019). [28]

London Waste and Recycling Board (2019), *Circular Economy Investment for Businesses in London*, http://www.lwarb.gov.uk/what-we-do/circular-london/circular-economy-investment-for-businesses/ (accessed on 5 August 2019). [19]

London Waste and Recycling Board (2019), *London Waste and Recycling Board Website*, http://www.lwarb.gov.uk/ (accessed on 6 June 2019). [16]

Ministry for Ecological Transition and the Demographic Challenge (2020), *El Gobierno declara la emergencia climática*, https://www.miteco.gob.es/es/prensa/200121cmindeclaracionemergencia_tcm30-506549.pdf (accessed on 26 February 2020). [4]

Ministry for Ecological Transition and the Demographic Challenge (2018), *Información pública de la estrategia Española de Economía Circular 12/02/18*, https://www.miteco.gob.es/es/calidad-y-evaluacion-ambiental/participacion-publica/Residuos-2018-Nota-sobre-proceso-informacion-publica-estrategia-espanola-economia-circular.aspx (accessed on 26 February 2020). [2]

Ministry of Development (2019), "Agenda Urbana Española", http://www.aue.gob.es/sites/aue/files/aue_doc_completo_21_02_2019_0.pdf (accessed on 29 November 2019). [5]

Ministry of Presidency, R. (2020), *Boletin Oficial del Estado - Real Decreto 2/2020, de 12 de enero, por el que se reestructuran los departamentos ministeriales*, https://www.boe.es/eli/es/rd/2020/01/12/2/con (accessed on 26 February 2020). [60]

Natural Heritage of Castile and León (2018), "La Fundación, como integrante de la red europea GPP NGO European Network organizó un curso sobre contratación pública verde y circular", https://patrimonionatural.org/noticias/general/2018/12/20/la-fundacion-como-integrante-de-la-red-europea-gpp-ngo-european-network-organizo-un-curso-sobre-contratacion-publica-verde-y-circular (accessed on 21 January 2020). [13]

OECD (2020), *A Territorial Approach to the Sustainable Development Goals: Synthesis Report*, OECD Urban Policy Reviews, OECD Publishing, Paris, https://dx.doi.org/10.1787/e86fa715-en. [10]

OECD (2019), *OECD Highlights of the 1st OECD Roundtable on the Circular Economy in Cities and Regions*, OECD, Paris. [20]

OECD (2019), *OECD Survey on the Circular Economy in Cities and Regions*, OECD, Paris. [32]

OECD (2016), *Water Governance in Cities*, https://www.oecd-ilibrary.org/governance/water-governance-in-cities_9789264251090-en (accessed on 6 February 2020). [26]

OECD (2013), *Scaling-up Finance Mechanisms for Biodiversity*, OECD Publishing, Paris, https://dx.doi.org/10.1787/9789264193833-en. [55]

OECD (2012), *Functional Urban Areas by Country*, OECD, Paris, https://www.oecd.org/cfe/regional-policy/functionalurbanareasbycountry.htm (accessed on 24 February 2020). [11]

OECD (forthcoming), *The Circular Economy in Cities and Regions*, Synthesis Report, OECD Publishing, Paris. [8]

Paris Municipality (2017), *Paris Circular Economy Plan 2017-2020*, https://api-site-cdn.paris.fr/images/97397 (accessed on 11 June 2019). [45]

San Sebastian City Council (2016), "Aprobada la bonificación del 15% en la tasa de basura por utilizar el quinto contenedor", http://www.donostia.eus/home.nsf/0/DD2431ECEA04493EC1257F4D004D1232?OpenDocument&idioma=cas (accessed on 5 June 2019). [57]

SmartEnCity (2019), *SmartEnCity.eu*, https://smartencity.eu/about/ (accessed on 30 April 2019). [59]

The Circular Lab (2019), *Homepage*, http://www.thecircularlab.com (accessed on 7 June 2019). [37]

UN (2019), *Goal 12: Sustainable Development Knowledge Platform*, United Nations, https://sustainabledevelopment.un.org/sdg12 (accessed on 7 February 2020). [9]

University of Valladolid (2019), *Homepage*, http://comunicacion.uva.es/export/sites/comunicacion/98240de9-350c-11e9-b081-d59857eb090a/ (accessed on 7 June 2019). [40]

Urban Agenda Partnership for Circular Economy (2020), *The Circular City Funding Guide*, European Investment Bank, https://www.circularcityfundingguide.eu/ (accessed on 6 February 2020). [21]

Valladolid Chamber of Commerce (2019), *Masters and Postgraduate Courses 2018-2019*, http://www.escueladenegocio.com/eden/wp-content/uploads/2018/08/Cat%C3%A1logo-Masters-y-Cursos-de-Postgrado-2018-2019.pdf (accessed on 11 June 2019). [31]

Valladolid City Council (2018), *Subvenciones para Economía Circular y Ecoinnovación*, http://www.valladolidadelante.es/node/12578 (accessed on 6 June 2019). [22]

Valladolid Municipality (2019), "39 proyectos de economía circular se ponen en marcha en Valladolid con el apoyo del Ayuntamiento", http://www.valladolidadelante.es/node/13384 (accessed on 6 June 2019). [23]

Valladolid Municipality (2019), "El Ayuntamiento de Valladolid consigue tres nuevos proyectos con financiación europea", http://www.valladolidadelante.es/node/13414 (accessed on 11 June 2019). [25]

Valladolid Municipality (2018), "El Ayuntamiento y Ecoembes impulsan un proyecto piloto de economía circular para lograr el correcto depósito del 60% de los residuos en un año", http://www.valladolid.es/es/actualidad/noticias/ayuntamiento-ecoembes-impulsan-proyecto-piloto-economia-cir (accessed on 7 June 2019). [39]

Valladolid Municipality (2018), *Valladolid Roadmap towards a Circular Economy*. [24]

Valladolid Municipality (2017), *Plan municipal de vivienda de Valladolid*, http://www.smviva.com/anexos/430/1496745970.pdf (accessed on 11 June 2019). [47]

Valladolid Municipality (2015), *Ayuntamiento de Valladolid suprime la tasa de basuras y congela el resto de tributos para 2016*, https://www.valladolid.es/es/actualidad/noticias/ayuntamiento-valladolid-suprime-tasa-basuras-congela-resto- (accessed on 29 November 2019). [35]

VITARTIS (2019), *Estrategia de Bioeconomía para la Industria Alimentaria de Castilla y León - BioEconomIA*, https://www.vitartis.es/portfolio-item/estrategia-de-bioeconomia-para-la-industria-alimentaria-de-castilla-y-leon-bioeconomia/ (accessed on 2 August 2019). [30]

Notes

[1] Ministry of the Presidency and Territorial Administrations; Ministry of Energy, Tourism and Digital Agenda; Ministry of Employment and Social Security; Ministry of Home Affairs; Ministry of Economy, Industry and Competitiveness; Tax Office and Public Function; Ministry of Health, Social Services and Equality; Ministry of Agriculture and Fisheries, Food and Environment; and Ministry of Publics Works.

[2] The new composition is the following: Ministry of Agriculture, Fisheries and Food; Ministry for Ecological Transition and the Demographic Challenge; Ministry of Economic Affairs and Digital Transformation; Ministry of Education and Vocational Training; Ministry of Finance; Ministry of Health; Ministry of Industry, Trade and Tourism; Ministry of the Interior; Ministry of Labour and Social Economy; Ministry of Presidency, Relations with Parliament and Democratic Memory; Ministry of Science and Innovation; Ministry of Territorial Policy and Civil Service; Ministry of Transports, Mobility and Urban Agenda; and Ministry of Universities (Ministry of Presidency, 2020[60]).

[3] For more information: www.eib.org/en/efsi/index.htm.

[4] For more information: www.eib.org/en/products/blending/innovfin/.

[5] *Reglamento Municipal de Limpieza, Recogida y Eliminación de Residuos Sólidos Urbanos del Ayuntamiento de Valladolid and Ordenanza Municipal de Protección del Medio Urbano del citado Ayuntamiento.*

[6] For more information: https://www.valladolid.es/es/ayuntamiento/ordenanzas-fiscales/ordenanzas-fiscales-2013/ordenanza-fiscal-tasa-reguladora-servicio-recogida-residuos.

[7] For more information: www.boe.es/buscar/pdf/1997/BOE-A-1997-8875-consolidado.pdf.

[8] An example of existing environmental certifications is the ISO 14001 "Environmental Management System". It provides practical tools for companies and organisations of all kinds looking to manage their environmental responsibilities in order to achieve the necessary requirements to get the certification https://www.iso.org/iso-14001-environmental-management.html.

[9] The "lighthouse" cities are part of the EU Horizon 2020 project "SmartEnCity" which aims to develop a highly adaptable and replicable systemic approach for transforming European cities into sustainable, smart

and resource-efficient urban environments. Other cities involved in the project are Sonderborg in Denmark, Tartu in Estonia and Vitoria-Gasteiz in Spain (SmartEnCity, 2019[59]).

[10] Two projects are ongoing: "Habitarte", a contest on eco-design of equipment for buildings for collective use; and "Eco design 4 Contract", a guide for the implementation of eco-design processes in the "contract industry" (a growing example of the *product-as-a-service* business model that provides furniture as a service through signing a contract and providing all the furniture needed in an apartment for an agreed period of time) (AEICE, 2019[48]).

[11] For more information: https://www.fiarebancaetica.coop/.

[12] For more information: https://www.triodos.es/es.

[13] For more information: http://web.finnovaregio.org/.

3 Policy recommendations and actions for a circular economy in Valladolid, Spain

In response to the challenges identified in Chapter 2, this chapter suggests some policy recommendations to implement the circular economy in the city of Valladolid, Spain. The policy recommendations are accompanied by a list of actions for concrete implementation, according to international practices.

Introduction

A total of 19 recommendations have been identified accordingly to the role of the city as promoter, facilitator and enabler of the circular economy (Table 3.1). These recommendations are accompanied by a set of actions aiming at supporting Valladolid's transition to a circular economy. The proposed actions are indicative and based on international practices while taking into account the local context. These international practices carried out in the field of the circular economy by cities, regions and national governments can serve as inspiration for the implementation of the recommendations. As such, they are not expected to be replicated in Valladolid but rather provide the municipality with a set of examples for the development and implementation of the suggested actions.

Table 3.1. Policy recommendations for the circular economy in Valladolid, Spain

Promoter	Facilitator	Enabler
Carry out urban metabolism analyses	Co-ordinate the local roadmap with other strategies at the regional and national levels, in order to maximise synergies and collaborations	Identify the regulatory instruments that need to be adapted to foster the transition to a circular economy
Develop a circular economy strategy with clear objectives and measurable targets	Connect the local government with universities, businesses and citizens	Identify fiscal and economic tools for the circular economy
Map circular jobs in the city by sector	Support business development and stimulate entrepreneurship in the circular economy	Strengthen the role of the Agency of Innovation and Economic Development
Promote the "circular vision" "leading by example"	Strengthen the exchange of experiences with neighbouring cities	Implement Green Public Procurement
Strengthen the circular community		Develop training programmes on the circular economy
Raise awareness of the opportunities and tools to advance towards a circular economy		Enable small-scale initiatives
Introduce a certification or a label for "circular companies" as an incentive for local businesses		Strengthen the effectiveness of the municipal grants related to the circular economy
		Develop a monitoring and evaluation framework

It is important to note that:

- <u>Actions are neither compulsory nor binding</u>: Identified actions address a variety of ways to implement and achieve objectives. However, they are neither compulsory nor binding. They represent suggestions, for which adequacy and feasibility should be carefully evaluated by the municipality of Valladolid in an inclusive manner, involving stakeholders as appropriate. In turn, the combination of more than one action can be explored, if necessary.

- <u>Prioritisation of actions should be considered</u>: Taking into account the unfeasibility of addressing all recommendations at the same time, prioritisation is key. As such, steps taken towards a circular transition should be progressive.

- <u>Resources for implementation should be assessed</u>: The implementation of actions will require human, technical and financial resources. When prioritising and assessing the adequacy and feasibility of the suggested actions, the resources needed to put them in practice should be carefully evaluated, as well as the role of stakeholders that can contribute to the implementation phase.

- <u>The proposed actions should be updated in the future</u>: New potential steps and objectives may emerge as actions start to be implemented.

- Several stakeholders should contribute to their implementation: Policy recommendations and related actions should be implemented as a shared responsibility across a wide range of actors. The stakeholder groups contributing to this report and to the identification of the actions are represented in Figure 3.1. They have a key role as "do-ers" of the circular economy system in Valladolid, Spain, along with other stakeholders that will be engaged in the future.

Figure 3.1. Stakeholders map in Valladolid, Spain

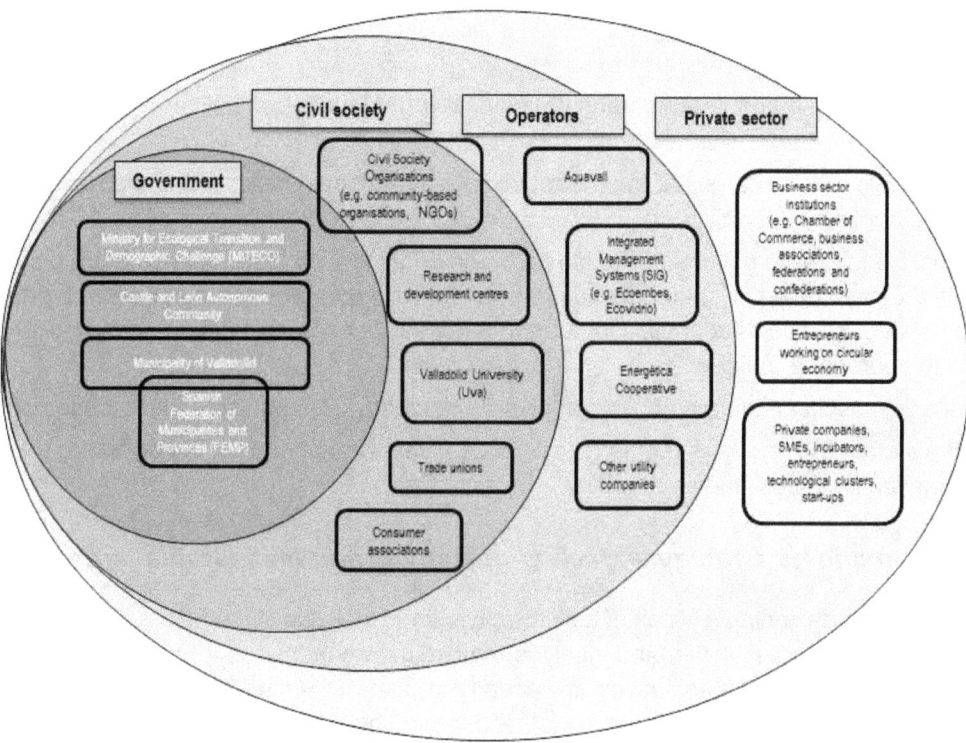

Note: This stakeholder's map is based on the 48 stakeholders that took part in the 2 OECD missions to the city of Valladolid on 25-28 February 2019 and 29 October 2019.

The city of Valladolid can play a role as promoter, facilitator and enabler of the circular economy strategy. Cities act as *promoters* when they identify priorities, promote concrete projects and engage stakeholders; they are *facilitators* when fostering co-operation between stakeholders, citizens and levels of government. The city's *enabler* role entails setting the necessary conditions for the circular economy (e.g. updating regulatory frameworks, catalysing funds, etc.). In order to boost the circular economy in Valladolid, the municipality could implement the recommendations detailed in this section.

Promoting a vision and a strategy for the circular economy

The city of Valladolid shows a strong willingness to start the journey towards a circular economy with a dedicated team, available funds and a community of circular economy entrepreneurs. These are relevant conditions to promote the circular economy in the city. In order to boost the circular economy in Valladolid, the municipality could implement the recommendations detailed in this section.

Carry out urban metabolism analyses

Urban metabolism analyses would aim to: i) develop knowledge on the material flows of the city to eventually reduce resource input extraction and negative externalities like pollution and waste (output); ii) reuse materials, when possible; iii) identify city's priorities based on the analysis of consumption and production trends. The municipality could co-operate with the university to carry out the analysis, which should be regularly updated and carried out at metropolitan and regional scale. The urban metabolism study in Paris could be taken as an example (Circular Metabolism, 2017[1]).

> *Key actions:*
>
> - Engage with universities and research and development (R&D) centres for the urban metabolism analysis.
> - Evaluate the scale of the analysis at the metropolitan and regional levels, with the collaboration of competent authorities.
> - Identify concrete follow-up actions to reduce resource consumption and negative output, such as pollution. In the case of water, materials and energy, for example, digital solutions can be applied (e.g. water meters, mobile data applications for mobility solutions, applications for energy saving), in addition to appropriate policies.
> - Disseminate the results of the metabolism analysis and clearly communicate them to the public.
> - Conduct the metabolism analysis regularly (e.g. once a year or biannually), in addition to updating environmental and climatic studies regularly.

Develop a circular economy strategy with clear objectives and measurable targets

A circular city would require designing a vision of how the city should look like in the future. A circular vision for the city entails refraining from a view that conceives the circular economy as a way of optimising the present linear system. Even if several initiatives are already in place in Valladolid, they are fragmented and, as such, it is difficult to determine relevant social, economic and environmental impacts. An overall vision would help to enhance coherence across different initiatives. This implies mapping sectors that apply circular economy principles and finding synergies across them, in order to avoid policy silos or short-term solutions. The strategy should make sure that the activities within the circular economy lead to a rethinking of production and consumption models and collaborations along the value chain. Examples of circular economy strategies at the subnational level are presented in Table 3.2. Once established, measurable targets should be linked to the objectives. Some measurement frameworks for the circular economy, applied at the city level, include the following: *Measuring the Circular Economy Developing an indicator set for Opportunity Peterborough* (Morley, Looi and Zhao, 2018[2]), *Indicators for a Circular Economy* (Vercalsteren, Christis and Van Hoof, 2018[3]), *Circular Economy Framework Monitoring Report*, Greater Porto Area, Portugal (LIPOR, 2018[4]).

Table 3.2. Circular economy initiatives at the subnational level

City	Country	Initiative
Amsterdam	Netherlands	Amsterdam Circular 2020-25 (2019)
Barcelona Metropolitan Area (AMB)	Spain	Circular economy promotion programme AMB circular (2019): i) Industrial Symbiosis Metropolitan Project ii) Platform of Natural Resources

City	Country	Initiative
		iii) Circular Economy Table
Brussels Capital Region	Belgium	Regional Programme for the Circular Economy 2016-20 (PREC)
Flanders	Belgium	Circular Flanders, 2016
Nantes	France	Circular Economy Roadmap Nantes (2018) (*Feuille de route économie circulaire Nantes Métropole*)
Paris	France	Circular Economy Plan 2017-20 (2017) (*Plan économie circulaire de Paris 2017-20*)
Rotterdam	Netherlands	Rotterdam Circularity Programme 2019-23
Scotland	United Kingdom	Making Things Last: A Circular Economy Strategy for Scotland (2016)
Tilburg	Netherlands	Tilburg Circular Agenda 2019

Source: OECD (forthcoming[5]), *The Circular Economy in Cities and Regions*, Synthesis Report, OECD Publishing, Paris.

Key actions:

Map existing circular initiatives in various sectors

- Identify key sectors (e.g. urban regeneration, tourism, construction, waste, etc.) that could generate relevant economic, environmental and social impacts, establish priorities and possible collaborations.
- Identify activities that can be relevant in shifting from a linear to a circular system (e.g. eco-design, services rather than ownership).

Define goals and actions

- Define result-oriented and realistic objectives, over the short, medium and long terms (e.g. circular economy-related projects, number of circular buildings to be constructed, etc.).
- Align the objectives of the circular economy strategy with the goals of existing policies (e.g. energy transition, climate change, smart city and urban planning).

Engage stakeholders

The circular economy is a shared responsibility across stakeholders that need to be involved from the phase zero of the strategy to build consensus and vision. Steps consist of (OECD, 2015[6]):

- Designing a participative methodology to engage key stakeholders to work on the definition and co-creation of a circular economy strategy that reflects their concerns:
  - Map all stakeholders that have a stake in the outcome or are likely to be affected, as well as their responsibility, core motivations and interactions.
  - Define the ultimate line of decision-making, the objectives of stakeholder engagement and the expected use of input.
  - Use stakeholder engagement techniques, ensuring the effective representation of all stakeholders in the process.
  - Allocate proper financial and human resources and share needed information for result-oriented stakeholder engagement.
  - Regularly assess the process and outcomes of stakeholder engagement to learn, adjust and improve accordingly.

- o Embed engagement processes in clear legal and policy frameworks, organisational structures/principles and responsible authorities.
- o Customise the type and level of engagement to the needs and keeping the process flexible to changing circumstances.
- o Clarify how the inputs will be used.
- o Communicate clearly on the responsibility of each actor in the municipality.
- Organising communication campaigns and activities in the city to raise awareness among stakeholders on the circular economy's objectives and benefits and how citizens can contribute.
- Creating participation spaces for citizens and stakeholders throughout the different implementation phases of the circular economy strategy. Instruments for stakeholders engagement include:
  - o Multi-stakeholder fora.
  - o Workshops.
  - o Breakfast meetings on the circular economy.
  - o Co-creation methodologies.
  - o Feedback loops.

Develop a financial plan

- Design a set of actions for the achievement of objectives, define their expected outcomes and allocate a budget and resources to each of the actions.
- Develop a financial plan for the implementation of the strategy
- Identify and communicate the costs (environmental, social and opportunity costs) and benefits of circular activities compared to linear approaches (baseline scenario or no action taken).

Monitoring and evaluation

- Identify indicators and measurable targets (economic, social and environmental ones) to monitor and evaluate the strategy. The indicator proposed by the OECD (forthcoming[5]) can be taken into account:

Setting the strategy
- o No. of public administrations/departments involved in the design of the circular economy startegy.
- o No. of actions identified to achieve the objectives.
- o No. of circular economy projects to implement the actions.
- o No. of staff employed for the circular economy strategy's design within the city/region/administration.
- o No. of stakeholders involved to co-create the circular economy strategy.
- o No. of projects financed by the city/regional government/Total number of projects.
- o No. of projects financed by the private sectors/Total number of projects.

Implementing the strategy
- o Waste diverted from landfill (T/inhabitant/year or %).
- o CO_2 emission avoided (T CO_2/capita or %).
- o Raw material avoided (T/inhabitant/year or %)/
- o Use of recovered material (T/inhabitant/year or %).
- o Energy savings (Kgoe/inhabitant/year or %).

- o Water savings (ML/inhabitant/year or %).
- Clearly communicate the aim and the expected outputs of the strategy.

Map circular jobs in the city by sector

The circular economy vision could also map possible opportunities for job creation, either from new activities or from changes in businesses, requiring adaptation. This could help to: i) obtain an overview of the future employment situation and detect the most vulnerable sectors; ii) match supply and demand in the job market in the city and its surrounding areas; and iii) set premises to adapt educational programmes and training to the needs of the circular economy transition, including for the business sector to include circularity in production processes and practices. Some approaches to circular jobs at the city level are presented in Box 3.1.

Box 3.1. City approaches to circular jobs

The circular economy transition holds the potential to generate new jobs. By 2035, the European Commission (EC) expects to create more than 170 000 new direct jobs related to the circular economy through the implementation of the Circular Economy Package. The International Labour Organization (ILO) estimates that by 2030, employment will grow the most in the services (50 million) and waste management (45 million) sectors worldwide (ILO, 2018[7]). Below some examples of how cities account for "circular" jobs are reported.

- In 2016, the city of **Paris** (France) has identified 66 500 full-time jobs related to the circular economy. Mostly, jobs are associated with energy management, renewable energies, waste incineration with energy recovery and part of the activities related to transport infrastructure. Moreover, 7 additional categories of activities are considered as related to the circular economy: eco-design, industrial and territorial ecology, the functional economy, sustainable supply, responsible consumption, extension of service life and recycling. The quantification of jobs is carried out via three approaches: by sector of activity (jobs in rental, repair, second-hand, transport, secondary raw material industries, waste collection with energy recovery); by type of products (e.g. recycled paper); by specific registered institutions (jobs that take place in institutions registered as Producer Responsibility Organisations, PRO).

- In 2013, the city of **London** (United Kingdom) counted 46 700 jobs in circular economy activities. Three types of jobs were considered in: recycling (wholesale of waste and scrap); reuse (repair of metal products, machinery and equipment; repair of computers, electronics and household goods; and retail sale of second-hand goods); and rental and leasing activities. The London Waste and Recycling Board (LWARB) showed that by 2030 sales and customer services jobs would increase by 1.18%, followed by medium-skilled (0.66%) and high-skilled ones (0.30%). The LWARB identifies three levels of job specialisation: i) high-skilled (e.g. managers, directors and senior officials, associate professional and technical positions); ii) medium-skilled (e.g. administrative and secretarial roles, skilled trade occupations and process, plant and machine operatives); iii) low-skilled (e.g. sales and customer services and elementary occupations.

- In 2016, the **Amsterdam Metropolitan Area** (AMA) (Netherlands) counted 140 000 jobs as part of the circular economy (11% of total jobs in the area). Digital technology, circular design and lifetime extension are the most relevant sectors. The AMA defined seven key circular elements for "directly circular jobs", divide in "core circular jobs" and "enabling circular jobs". "Core circular jobs" are related to activities that prioritise regenerative resources (e.g. renewable energy sector); preserve and extend what is already made (e.g. repair sector); use waste as a resource (e.g. recycling); and rethink business models (e.g. renting or leasing activities). The "enabling circular jobs" aim to create joint value from collaborations (e.g. professional and networking associations); design for the future (e.g. architecture or industrial design); and incorporate digital technology (e.g. digital innovation). "Indirectly circular jobs" are also identified and refer to all other sectors that offer services to circular jobs activities and that create supporting circular activities (e.g. education, government and professional services). Six groups of skills relevant to future circular jobs are: basic skills (capacities that facilitate acquiring new knowledge); complex problem solving (abilities to solve new, complex problems in real-world settings); resource management skills (capacities for efficient resource allocation); social skills (abilities to work with people towards achieving common goals); systems skills (capacities to understand, evaluate and enhance "socio-technical systems"); and technical skills (competencies to design, arrange, use and repair machines and technological systems).

There are also examples of indicators to measure job creation:

- In **Peterborough** (United Kingdom), "Circular Peterborough" the local circular economy programme developed eight indicators that include socioeconomic dimensions, one of which measure the "percentage of circular jobs and percentage of circular business". The *Measuring the Circular Economy – Developing an indicator set for Opportunity Peterborough* report details six sub-indicators to measure the "percentage of circular economy jobs" in the city: retail of second-hand goods in stores; rental and leasing activities; wholesale of waste and scrap; waste collection activities and repair of computers and household goods; repair and installation of machinery.

- The city of **Toronto** (Canada) measures the social dimension of the circular economy through three indicators: the number of green jobs created and secured, the number of city staff trained on circular procurement principles and the asset/sharing utilisation activities.

Source: EC (2016[8]), *Circular Economy Package: Four Legislative Proposals on Waste*, European Commission; ILO (2018[9]), *World Employment and Social Outlook 2018 – Greening with Jobs*, http://www.ilo.org/publns (accessed on 29 January 2020); City of Paris (2019[10]), *Quantifier les emplois de l'économie circulaire de Paris - Synthèse*; LWARB (2017[11]), *Employment and the Circular Economy: Job Creation through Resource Efficiency in London*, http://www.wrap.org.uk (accessed on 29 January 2020); Circle Economy/ EHERO (2018[12]), *Circular Jobs and Skills in the Amsterdam Metropolitan Area*, https://assets.website-files.com/5d26d80e8836af7216ed124d/5d26d80e8836af6ddeed12a2 (accessed on 5 February 2020); Morley, A., E. Looi and C. Zhao (2018[2]), *Measuring the Circular Economy: Developing an Indicator Set for Opportunity Peterborough*; City of Toronto (2018[13]), *Circular Economy Procurement Implementation Plan and Framework*.

Key actions:

- Carry out specific studies to identify future job opportunities in the city by sector:
    - Develop consultation activities with representatives of various sectors, from retails to hospitality and services, to understand the level of circularity across the value chains and identify gaps and job opportunities.
    - Analyse the type of skills required, from low- to high-qualification and competency levels by sector.
    - Strengthen the artisanal sector for products reuse.
    - Match the financial, human and technical capacities with the identified needs.
- Explore the possibility of incorporating the circular economy as a new topic of work into the ongoing social dialogue between the city of Valladolid, business sector institutions and trade unions.

Promote the "circular vision" "leading by example"

The municipality could start to apply circular principles in its activities and services to lead by example. The municipality should be an example of change and make this an explicit target, in order to: i) show the feasibility of moving towards a circular transition through specific actions; ii) "practice what you preach" through concrete examples and activities; iii) raise public awareness of the impacts of the circular economy. This could be done, for example, through: reducing waste generation (banning one-use plastics like cups in municipal events and daily activities); applying the product-as-a-service model through public procurement (paying for a lighting service adapted to the municipality's needs rather than buying light bulbs and appliances); and promoting the use of secondary materials. Since 2015, Amsterdam, Netherlands has been implementing the "Learning by doing" programme that aims to show with empirical examples that the circular economy is profitable in all aspects by gathering different city departments and diverse stakeholders to define policy actions. Regarding new business models based on renting and sharing, the following examples can be provided: Amsterdam Airport Schiphol rents light as a service, instead of the traditional model of buying light bulbs: with this model, Schiphol pays for the light it uses while Philips continues to be the owner of all installations and is responsible for their performance and durability (Circular Economy Club, 2019[14]). The city of Tokyo, Japan, aims to reduce CO_2 emissions produced during celebration of the 2020 Olympic Games by renting and leasing materials, saving resources, minimising waste production and using recycled materials for stakeholders' uniforms, among other measures (Organising Committee of the Olympic and Paralympic Games Tokyo 2020, 2018[15]).

Key actions:

- Apply circular models within the municipality and communicate them clearly to the citizens. Examples of these practices could include:
    - Green Public Procurement (GPP): award criteria favouring the transition to a circular economy (e.g. reuse, durability, reparability, purchase of second-hand or remanufactured products).
    - Business models that would shift from ownership to services (e.g. product-as-a-service model through public procurement: pay for a lighting service adapted to the municipality's needs rather than buying light bulbs and appliances; lease a furniture service instead of buying specific furniture, etc.).
    - Reduction of waste generation (e.g. plans to prevent waste production; reducing the use of paper or banning one-use plastics like cups in municipal events and daily activities).
    - Provision of the required containers for separate collection throughout the city.
- Clearly communicate to citizens goals, all the circular initiatives that are being promoted by the city and the progress achieved (e.g. percentage of one-use plastic avoided in one year, etc.).

Strengthen the circular community

Thanks to the municipal grants dedicated to the circular economy, there is a growing circular community in Valladolid. It is important, therefore, to build momentum and make sure that the community can be strengthened. This would reinforce the commitment to the transition to a circular economy in various sectors; reduce potential resistances to change to the traditional model of the linear economy and increase citizen awareness of the circular economy. Several tools could be used, such as furthering communication instruments (online and offline platforms to promote projects and initiatives), and creating spaces for meetings and dialogues. For example, an online platform dedicated to the circular economy where different stakeholders can share information on events and experiences could be a way of promoting synergies among them. The online platform should be managed and moderated by an identified reliable entity.

Key actions:

- Create a circular economy forum, led by the Agency of Innovation and Economic Development, establishing a dialogue between citizens, businesses, entrepreneurs (that have responded to the call for municipal grants or new companies).
- Create a permanent working group or committee composed by different stakeholders (private sector, public administration, unions, business associations, etc.) to propose ideas and exchange experiences. Include a calendar of meetings to guarantee the continuity.
- Create an online platform or website with clear and accessible information on existing tools and future opportunities. The online platform should be a dynamic and living tool managed and moderated by an identified and trustable entity (e.g. the Agency of Innovation and Economic Development).
- Explore the possibility of establishing a "circular economy pact" in the city, between businesses and local entities, similar to the circular economy pact established at the national level.
- Identify incentives, awards and challenges by neighbours to stimulate new ideas and motivate the circular community.

Raise awareness of the opportunities and tools to advance towards a circular economy

It is key to provide examples of successful business cases (e.g. in terms of cost-saving and job creation). One way to do so would be through "circular economy ambassadors". The city of London, through its Waste and Recycling Board, has started recruiting "circular economy ambassadors" in different companies and local authorities to share information on the benefits of the circular economy for each economic sector and to raise awareness in the workplace (London Waste and Recycling Board, 2017[16]). Architects, urbanists, artists and environmentalists could also offer examples of good practices and multidisciplinary approaches. Another instrument could be the creation of a platform as a marketplace where companies could exchange, sell and buy products and reusable materials. A similar practice is carried out in the city of Austin (United States) through the Austin Materials Marketplace, which is an entirely digital platform.

Key actions:

- Several tools can be considered:
  - Communication campaigns to show the impacts of the circular economy and to explain how citizens and different stakeholders can contribute to it. These campaigns could include real experiences from actors that have already incorporated the circular economy in their processes.
  - Conferences and seminars at schools and universities in order to raise awareness among children and students in Valladolid.
  - Dedicated website in order to share knowledge, good practices by sector concerning the circular economy (e.g. create a digital repository of circular economy projects in Valladolid).
  - Events for knowledge sharing, networking and the promotion of the circular economy.
  - Social media to update on current initiatives.
- Incorporate programmes of healthy habits in the circular economy strategy when suitable (e.g. consumption, elimination of food waste, healthy urbanism, among others).
- Consider introducing the figure of "circular economy ambassadors" in the municipality, the private sector and civil society (e.g. companies, local entities, unions) as the delegates responsible for sharing information on the impacts of the circular economy.

- Create environmental delegates (*delegados de medio ambiente*) in work councils (*comités de empresa*) incorporating circular economy topics under their responsibilities.
- Explore tools for favouring reuse and create a circular "culture", such as:
    - Platforms for exchanging used good and materials (e.g. furniture, textiles, clean points, etc.).
    - Fairs and events for the exchange of used goods.
    - Applications for the exchange of used goods.
    - Platforms of industry by-products by sector to facilitate inter-company circularity.

Introduce a certification or a label for "circular companies" as an incentive for local businesses

The municipality could consider introducing a certification or a label for companies following circular principles, in order to: help consumers to distinguish companies that are embracing circular economy principles; promote the adoption of circular economy models in the transformation processes of private companies; identify materials produced and used in a circular manner and reward circular companies and incentivise others to start their transition. There are several examples of labels and certificates granted when products are produced locally, with little or no packaging, energy consumption is reduced, waste properly treated according to the best available option, etc. (Box 3.2). Criteria for labelling could be formulated following detailed studies by universities and research centres while incorporating the view of local retailer shops.

Box 3.2. Examples of labelled products for the circular economy

Certifications are made to assure stakeholders and clients that products and services meet requirements linked to the circular economy. Both the private sector and national and local authorities are taking steps in this regard to develop and introduce labels for the circular economy:

- **OrganiTrust®,** a worldwide certification body, issues certificates on the circular economy in the following sectors: food contact material, personal care and cosmetics, furniture, children toys, textiles and fabrics, electronics, building materials, medical safety equipment and household chemicals and detergents. In addition, it also provides this qualification to some service activities, which include transport, construction, telecommunications, cleaning and parking. Once the product or service has achieved the certification, it must be renewed annually.
- The **Amsterdam Made** certificate was developed upon request of the Amsterdam City Council. Its main objective consists in informing consumers about products that are made in the Amsterdam area, while simultaneously seeking to boost creativity, innovation, sustainability and craftsmanship.
- The French roadmap for the circular economy, **50 Measures for a 100% Circular Economy**, launched by the Ministry for an Ecological and Solidary Transition *(Ministère de la Transition écologique et solidaire)* in 2018, includes the deployment of voluntary environmental labelling in 5 pilot sectors (furnishing, textile, hotels, electronic products and food products).
- The **White Paper on the Circular Economy of Greater Paris** (Mairie de Paris, 2015[17]) contemplates 65 proposals, including the design and use of circular economy labels. More precisely, it aims to provide higher visibility of existing environmental labels in France, such as NF Environment (a collective certification label for producers who comply with environmental quality specifications) and the European ecolabel, as well as the development of a quality label for second-hand products.

Source: French Government (2018[18]), *50 Measures for a 100% Circular Economy*, http://www.ecologique-solidaire.gouv.fr/sites/default/files/FREC%20-%20EN.pdf (accessed on 6 June 2019); Amsterdam Made (2019[19]), *Homepage*, http://www.amsterdammade.org/en/ (accessed on 6 June 2019); Mairie de Paris (2015[17]), *White Paper on the Circular Economy of Greater Paris*, https://api-site.paris.fr/images/77050 (accessed on 11 June 2019); Organi Trust (2019[20]), *Circular Economy and Organic Certification*, https://organitrust.org/ (accessed on 11 June 2019); HQE-GBC (2019[21]), *Circular Economy for HQE Sustainable Construction*.

Key actions:

- Strengthen existing eco-labelling in existing production processes amongst companies in Valladolid, by introducing circular economy principles and monitoring progress.
- Take into account the circular economy criteria for certification. For example:
    - Use of recycled materials.
    - Development of life-analysis calculations.
    - Deconstruction processes.
    - Presentation of a plan for materials reuse.
    - Extended product lifespan (e.g. long guarantee, availability of spare parts of a product to enable repairs).
    - Product-as-a-service concept.
- Based on the information of international experiences, prioritise certain sectors in order to undertake pilot experiments on circular certificates.
- Collaborate with local universities and research centres to analyse the criteria for circular certifications.
- Define common guidelines for circular economy products and processes at a local level in order to obtain the certification.
- Promote systematic recognition of good practices through audits.
- Promote the development of activities to enhance the use and the value of certifications (e.g. a materials bank).

Facilitating multilevel co-ordination for the circular economy

The municipality can facilitate collaborations and co-operation among a wide range of actors to make the circular economy happen on the ground. Possible actions the city could apply are described below.

Co-ordinate the local roadmap with other strategies at the regional and national levels, in order to maximise synergies and collaborations

This recommendation aims at fostering policy coherence across different strategies/roadmaps that may concern various sectors, from food to mobility to land use, and that have common objectives, from waste reduction to climate neutrality. Therefore, linking existing strategies at the regional and national levels can enable the local government to achieve common goals, while identifying synergies. For example, the Brussels Region Regional Programme for the Circular Economy 2016-20 is co-ordinated by three ministers and four regional administrative bodies (Region of Brussels, 2016[22]); the Public Waste Agency of Flanders (OVAM), took the initiative in 2018 to set up a national platform for the circular economy, through which the top levels of federal and regional environment departments, economy/innovation departments and finance departments meet twice a year to decide on common action in priority policy fields (OECD, forthcoming[5]).

Key actions:

- Identify existing strategies and related targets than can be achieved through the circular economy (e.g. UN Agenda 2030 for Sustainable Development, Paris Climate Agreement).
- Identify synergies across existing and upcoming strategies of the city (e.g. climate change, housing, energy, urban planning, etc.) to incorporate circular economy principles.
- Identify circular economy initiatives available at the regional and national levels and the role of the city in contributing to the achievement of goals.
- Create co-ordination platforms, for example:
    - Organise seminars and workshops, ad hoc meetings to align interests across local, regional and national authorities.
    - Circular economy network that includes representatives from the municipalities of Castile and León, the region and the national government.
    - Co-operation agreements between Valladolid, the Castile and León Autonomous Community and other municipalities of the region for the implementation of joint projects on the circular economy.
    - Explore the opportunities derived from contracts/deals with the regional and the national government as tools for dialogue, for experimenting, empowering and learning.

Connect the local government with universities, businesses and citizens

Improving co-ordination among key stakeholders would build knowledge on the circular economy, as well as achieve a set of shared, achievable and realistic objectives. For example, academic research could be related to local needs towards a circular economy transition and connected with the local productive ecosystem of small- and medium-sized enterprises (SMEs). This could be also done through "challenges" and "open calls" to solve municipal issues and stimulate innovation. Some international examples can provide inspiration. For instance, Start-up in Residence (San Francisco, United States) and the Amsterdam Circular Challenge (Amsterdam, Netherlands) connect start-ups and businesses to provide solutions to city's problems through transparent selection processes.

Key actions:

- Identify possible pilots and experimentations that would involve R&D and university departments, based on the needs of the municipality (e.g. circular activities in the mobility, tourism, food, waste sector, bio-economy, etc.).
- Collect academic and business proposals to put in place circular activities with social impact and consider support for implementation (e.g. financial support for students).
- Collaboration agreements between the municipality and the university to work on prioritised areas related to the circular economy at the local level.
- Collaborate with universities to implement the circular economy in the existing educational programmes.
- Organise events, workshops and fairs, where companies can share their technology needs and find new partners.
- Create interactive online platforms to encourage stakeholders to exchange information with each other on their needs and monitor the activities and updates of the platform.

- Create co-working spaces for cross-fertilisation amongst several actors.
- Collaborate with businesses and unions to start or boost their transition to a circular economy. Include this matter in the social dialogue between the city, unions and businesses.

Support business development and stimulate entrepreneurship in the circular economy

The city can support businesses through regulatory, financial, and capacity building tools to provide conditions to stimulate circular businesses in start-up and existing companies. Some international practices are: Prodock, the scale-up incubator of the port of Amsterdam, which, since 2016, helps business and companies to co-create solutions in a shared working space in diverse topics, from transforming wet waste into renewable gas, to producing sustainable bio-based chemicals, or recycling plastic and soap waste in the hospitality sector. The London Waste and Recycling Board set up a programme called Advance London to start up and scale up businesses related to the circular economy. Enriching consulting services offered to enterprises with a component on the circular economy practices could be another way to promote innovation (e.g. the Chamber of Commerce could do that or be actively involved). Moreover, facilitating dialogues on the circular economy's potential by sector across existing business clusters that bring together SMEs and knowledge centres could also promote new business models and innovation. It is key for experts in each sector (e.g. tourism, construction, waste, etc.) to share experiences to have a better understanding of what can be done, where the gaps are and how they can be overcome.

Key actions:

- A variety of tools have been identified from international practices, such as:
  - Tax breaks or social security exemptions for companies that perform environmentally relevant investments related to the circular economy (e.g. sustainable energy technologies such as energy recovery).
  - One-stop-shop for companies seeking information on circular business models and on regulation and legislation.
  - Platform to share concrete examples of successful cases and failures in circular business models.
  - Spaces for experimentation and sharing results.
  - Pre-incubation services to ensure that entrepreneurs have a reasonable chance of success and incubators to foster knowledge sharing and pilot testing.
  - Community building to facilitate peer learning.
- Establish collaboration with the Chamber of Commerce of Valladolid for ad hoc consultancy services, training and mentoring programmes.
- Explore ways to reduce the bureaucratic burdens for circular start-up and circular companies.

Strengthen the exchange of experiences with neighbouring cities

The city of Valladolid participates in several international projects that allow exchanges with European cities. Participating in city networks related to the circular economy and learning from other cities can be an important source of inspiration for Valladolid. This would include specific actions (e.g. return system for plastic bottles, door to door collection) and capacity building, training, communication initiatives. A network of neighbouring cities could be set up in order to investigate the potential of circular economy activities within the area, in which Valladolid could play a leading role, given its experience.

Key actions:

- Create spaces for dialogue and experience exchange, enhancing common actions and learning processes within the metropolitan area. These initiatives could include:
  - Events and workshops to exchange success stories, good practices and barriers.
  - Thematic partnerships that promote common actions across cities of the metropolitan area and within the region, where Valladolid can take a lead role, having advanced on a series of circular economy initiatives.
- Strengthen dialogues regarding the circular economy with the Provincial Council and the Federation of Municipalities and Provinces.
- Take actively part in city networks related to the circular economy, sharing knowledge and learning from other cities (regional, national and international levels).
- Monitor and participate in events related to the circular economy in cities.

Enabling the economics and governance conditions for the uptake of the circular economy

Implementing a circular economy entails enabling the necessary governance and economic conditions. As such, the city government could adopt the actions detailed in the following section.

Identify the regulatory instruments that need to be adapted to foster the transition to a circular economy

This includes investigating which tools can be used at the local level to enable the transition to the circular economy and those that need coordination with other levels of government. Regulatory instruments include: specific requirements for land use, environmental permits (e.g. for decentralised water, waste and energy systems), regulation for pilots and experimentation. For example, in the Netherlands, the legal and regulatory framework at the local and regional levels is expected to adapt to the National Circular Economy Strategy (OECD, forthcoming[5]).

Key actions:

- Identify the available regulatory tools (e.g. land use, urban planning, environmental permits, waste plan) that can allow the transition to a circular economy now and in the future.
- Identify regulatory gaps and obstacles, which may go beyond the local sphere as per the competency of other levels of governments.
- Identify platforms for dialogue in which the local government can exchange with the regional and the national ones about possible regulatory obstacles that cannot be dealt with at the local level, as well as on regulatory instruments that can encourage circular practices.
- Advise companies on circular economy-related legislation.
- Identify areas for opportunities to set specific requirements on energy use, water requirements, demolition, circular construction.

Identify fiscal and economic tools for the circular economy

There are several fiscal and economic tools that the city of Valladolid could consider applying to boost the circular economy. This includes local taxes, fiscal bonuses, incentives, etc. These tools can incentivise or disincentivise behaviours towards the circular economy, such as increasing separate collection of waste.

Actions can also improve access to finance for circular economy projects in the starting, implementation and scale-up phases. Some international experiences are the following: the Dutch Government's DIFTAR system is a scheme based on differentiated tariffs in order to provide incentives to improve waste separation at source (pay-as-you-throw); VAT reductions for companies working on circular economy projects in Shanghai (China) and for reused items (Sweden); discounts on waste fees for businesses in Milan (Italy) and San Francisco (United States).

Key actions:

- Map the measures that the municipality can adopt according to its fiscal competencies. A range of fiscal tools have been identified from international practices, such as:
    - Property tax according to the energy consumption of buildings.
    - Corporate income tax (e.g. based on the waste generation level, water and energy consumption, use of recycled materials as raw materials).
    - VAT reduction on products labelled as circular (e.g. easy to recycle and reuse, proximity).
    - Tax reductions on second-hand materials.
    - Discount on waste fees according to preselected criteria.
    - Differentiated tariffs for waste separation and recycling (e.g. pay-as-you-throw approach).
- Explore the possibility of updating municipal economic tools (e.g. grants) to foster a circular economy local model.

Strengthen the role of the Agency of Innovation and Economic Development

The Agency of Innovation and Economic Development should strengthen his role as key actor for the circular economy in the municipality and co-ordinator across municipal departments. It is important for stakeholders to identify a responsible entity to co-ordinate, organise and monitor the interaction between stakeholders participating in networking activities and the circular economy community in the city, or soon to be.

Key actions:

- Establish clear roles and responsibilities within the agency in co-ordination with municipal departments.
- Lead the co-creation process of Valladolid's circular economy strategy (e.g. organising meetings, engaging with stakeholders, defining the necessary steps to develop the strategy, etc.).
- Carry out marketing activities, increase advertising and improve communication with citizens and businesses (e.g. organising conferences and circular talks).
- Participate in networks focusing on the circular economy.
- Incorporate the circular economy into the formal responsibilities of the agency.
- Create a specific team in charge of circular economy-related topics.
- Match needs with resources (financial, technical and human).
- Evaluate the activity of the agency on a regular basis and improve as appropriate.
- Establish partnerships and collaboration with other institutional partners, as appropriate.

Implement Green Public Procurement

Green Public Procurement (GPP) is a fundamental tool for cities to foster the circular transition, reducing the environmental impacts of public purchases at the city level. GPP should promote eco-efficiency, eco-design and collaborative consumption. For example, the city of Ljubljana (Lithuania) included environmental requirements in its tenders; the city of Paris (France) adopted a scheme for responsible public procurement; the city of Toronto (Canada) set up a Circular Economy Procurement Implementation Plan and Framework to use its purchasing power as a driver for waste reduction, economic growth and social prosperity (City of Toronto, 2018[13]).

Key actions:

- Include circular principles in the technical specifications, procurement selection and award criteria, as well as in contract performance clauses (e.g. reuse, durability, reparability, second-hand or remanufactured products).
- Adapt the public procurement evaluation system by increasing the value of social and environmental ratings in comparison with the price criteria.
- Establish clear requirements in tenders in order to foster change in materials, quality and maintenance (e.g. use secondary materials in publicly purchased goods).
- Apply life cycle analysis and develop criteria to evaluate the life cycle of the assets used by each municipal service, and use them to perform analysis of infrastructure, solutions and suppliers to foster more sustainable solutions in municipal services.
- Provide training for staff of public institutions responsible for the inclusion of circular criteria in the specifications.

Develop training programmes on the circular economy

The aim of this recommendation is to provide entrepreneurs and employees with deeper knowledge and tools to succeed in their circular projects while enhancing knowledge to develop circular activities. This could be done in co-operation with the Chamber of Commerce to build capacities among entrepreneurs and small business managers and raise awareness of the potential of the circular economy and new business models. For instance, the Chamber of Commerce of Glasgow (United Kingdom) provides capacity building programmes for businesses aiming to transition to a circular economy (Zero Waste Scotland, 2019[23]).

Key actions:

- Collaborate with business associations, trade unions and the Chamber of Commerce of Valladolid, to co-create joint training programmes for entrepreneurs and employees, to boost the circular economy and new business models.
- Identify existing training and educational programmes at the university level or carried out by research centres and foundations to establish possible synergies and provide support if need be.

Enable small-scale initiatives

Identifying places, areas and communities to experiment and share tools among neighbours for developing small-scale initiatives can be a first step to foster change at the local level, test the viability of circular initiatives with a lower risk, stimulate the creation of new ideas and circular business models and share knowledge on circular economy practices. The project developed in the La Victoria neighbourhood can act as an example for this kind of initiatives (Box 2.5). Since 2010 in Paris, France, the Urban Lab has accompanied more than 200 experiments and consolidated a methodology to support effective experimentation in 4 main stages: i) the definition of the experimental project and its evaluation; ii) a search of the experimental site; iii) the deployment of experimentation; and iv) valuation and transformation. In order to facilitate access to these experimental sites, the Urban Lab has been working for 10 years, in the development of a legal framework that start-ups can refer to for the development of their projects (e.g. a model agreement for using publicly owned spaces for a fixed period of time) (Urban Lab, 2019[24]).

Key actions:

- Explore and identify places to implement and pilot initiatives at the neighbourhood level, such as:
  - Pilot projects to achieve waste separation targets, door-to-door collection systems, food waste reduction and reduction of waste production (e.g. intelligent containers).
  - Digital solutions to reduce water and energy consumption and water recycling in public buildings as well as commercial activities.
  - New business models, enhancing waste prevention, reducing resource consumption and fostering local consumption. This can be one by:
    - Promoting the sharing economy (e.g. for the use of tools and equipment).
    - Fostering the purchase of locally produced goods.
    - Encouraging remanufacturing, refurbishing and 3D repair services (e.g. for computer equipment, textiles and furniture).
    - Promoting reuse (e.g. second-hand markets, exchange of materials and goods).

Strengthen the effectiveness of the municipal grants related to the circular economy While the municipal grants for the circular economy have stimulated entrepreneurship in the circular economy in the city, some improvements can be considered to increase the effectiveness of funds. At the same time, alternative funding sources beyond municipal grants could be explored. Some examples from international practices are revolving funds and funding schemes in co-operation with private and semi-public financial institutions (e.g. banks, business funds) (Box 2.3).

Key actions:

- Identify and update a set of criteria that could help select the projects, based on previous calls and evaluate proposals received on the "scalability" of each project.
- Make a distinction across applicants, as private-sector and non-profit organisations have different means, resources and scope and can therefore be evaluated on the basis of specific criteria.
- Monitor and evaluate impacts achieved by funded projects and the type of collective benefits achieved, e.g. in social and environmental terms.
- Share information on funding opportunities after the end of the grant. Possible options could include: soft loans, alternative and non-bank sources of finance, crowdfunding, peer-to-peer lending, business angel networks and venture capital.
- Consider the possibility of applying external audits to the projects.

Develop a monitoring and evaluation framework

Identifying how "circular" the city is, what works, what does not and what can be improved is important to progress toward the transition to a circular economy. The OECD scoreboard on the circular economy in cities and regions can contribute to this. These proposed OECD indicators could add to the 16 existing sustainability indicators that the city has defined in 2016 regarding quality of life, mobility, air quality and pollution (Agenda 21, 2016[25]). The proposed OECD indicators for the evaluation of the circular economy strategy in cities and regions are detailed in Box 3.3.

Key actions:

- Identify available indicators and data for the monitoring of progress and assessment of the results of the circular economy strategy, such as those proposed by the OECD (forthcoming[5]).
- Repeat the evaluation every year.

Box 3.3. The proposed OECD Circular Economy Scoreboard for Cities and Regions

The proposed OECD Circular Economy Scoreboard for cities and regions consists of a self-assessment of key governance conditions to evaluate the level of advancement towards a circular economy in cities and regions. It is composed of 10 key dimensions, whose implementation governments and stakeholders can evaluate based on a scoreboard system, indicating the level of implementation of each dimension (Newcomer, In progress and Advanced).

Table 3.3. OECD Circular Economy Scoreboard for Cities and Regions

	Level of advancement		
	Newcomer	In progress	Advanced
Circular economy framework	The city/region is planning to develop a circular economy strategy but has not started yet.	The circular economy strategy is under development.	Existence of a circular economy strategy with specific goals and priorities, actions, sectors and a monitoring framework.
Co-ordination mechanisms	There are no co-ordination mechanisms in place but under development.	Existence of dialogues across levels of government but not focused on the circular economy.	Co-ordination mechanisms across levels of governments to set and implement a circular economy strategy or initiative are well established and functioning.
Policy coherence	The circular economy initiatives are still not aligned with other related policy areas (e.g. climate change, sustainable development and air quality).	The circular economy initiatives are aligned with some specific related policy areas (e.g. climate change, sustainable development and air quality) but they are still fragmented.	Existence of an overall policy coherence between circular economy initiatives and related policy areas (e.g. climate change, sustainable development and air quality).
Economy and finance	No current financial instruments in place but planned.	Existence of a budget dedicated to environmental spending that is foreseen to be used also for circular economy projects.	Existence of a funding programme and economic incentives for circular economy projects with specific objectives, prioritised sectors and a monitoring framework of the outcomes.
Innovation	There are no spaces to test and pilot but planned.	Design of spaces to test and pilot circular economy projects under development.	Existence of spaces to test and pilot circular economy projects.
Stakeholder engagement	Existence of an initiative for the mapping of the most relevant stakeholders in the city/region.	Existence of a dialogue with stakeholders for the design and implementation of the circular economy strategy.	Existence of participation spaces for stakeholders through which inputs are used for the design and implementation of circular strategies.
Capacity building	Existence of capacity building programmes on green and sustainable economy fields.	Existence of capacity building programmes for activities associated with designing, setting and implementing a circular economy initiative.	Regular capacity building programmes for activities associated with designing, setting, implementing and monitoring the circular economy strategy.
Green Public Procurement	Green Public Procurement is being developed.	Existence of a green procurement model including environmental criteria (e.g. reduction of CO_2 emissions).	Existence of a circular public procurement framework (e.g. waste diversion from procurement activities, raw materials avoided and percentage of recycled content).
Data and information	Identification of data on waste management and information campaigns to prevent waste generation.	Existence of data on waste management and information campaigns on the circular economy.	Existence of an information system on the circular economy. Data are publicly available and citizens and business informed of the opportunities related to circular business models and behaviours.
Monitoring and evaluation	No monitoring nor evaluation framework in place.	Existence of a monitoring and evaluation framework that includes environmental aspects.	Existence of a monitoring and evaluation framework that includes environmental, economic and social aspects.

> According to the self-evaluation, the city/region will identify its own level of advancement toward the transition to a circular economy, identify gaps and set its own targets for improvement. The methodology for self-assessment consists in a scoreboard system that can indicate the level of advancement of circular cities and regions towards the transition. Sub-indicators to better specify each dimension are under development and will be tested in the case studies of the OECD Programme on the Circular Economy in Cities and Regions.
>
> Source: OECD (forthcoming[5]), *The Circular Economy in Cities and Regions*, Synthesis Report, OECD Publishing, Paris.

References

Agenda 21 (2016), *Sustainability Indicators*, Valladolid's Local Agenda 21. [25]

Amsterdam Made (2019), *Homepage*, http://www.amsterdammade.org/en/ (accessed on 6 June 2019). [19]

Circle Economy/EHERO (2018), *Circular Jobs and Skills in the Amsterdam Metropolitan Area*, https://assets.website-files.com/5d26d80e8836af7216ed124d/5d26d80e8836af6ddeed12a2_Circle%20Economy%20-%20Circular%20Jobs%20and%20Skills%20in%20the%20Amsterdam%20Metropolitan%20Area.pdf (accessed on 5 February 2020). [12]

Circular Economy Club (2019), *Renting lighting: Schiphol Airport*, https://www.circulareconomyclub.com/solutions/renting-lighting-schiphol-airport/ (accessed on 21 February 2020). [14]

Circular Metabolism (2017), *The Circular Economy Plan of Paris*, https://www.circularmetabolism.com/input/11 (accessed on 3 December 2019). [1]

City of Paris (2019), *Quantifier les emplois de l'"économie circulaire de Paris - Synthèse*. [10]

City of Toronto (2018), *Circular Economy Procurement Implementation Plan and Framework*, https://www.toronto.ca/legdocs/mmis/2018/gm/bgrd/backgroundfile-115664.pdf. [13]

City of Toronto (2018), *Circular Economy Procurement Implementation Plan and Framework*. [28]

EC (2016), *Circular Economy Package: Four Legislative Proposals on Waste*, European Commission. [8]

French Government (2018), *50 Measures for a 100% Circular Economy*, http://www.ecologique-solidaire.gouv.fr/sites/default/files/FREC%20-%20EN.pdf (accessed on 6 June 2019). [18]

HQE-GBC (2019), *Circular Economy for HQE Sustainable Construction*. [21]

ILO (2018), *World Employment and Social Outlook 2018 – Greening with jobs*, International Labour Organization, http://www.ilo.org/publns (accessed on 29 January 2020). [9]

ILO (2018), *World Employment and Social Outlook 2018 – Greening with Jobs*, International Labour Organization, http://www.ilo.org/publns (accessed on 21 February 2020). [7]

LIPOR (2018), *Circular Economy Framework Monitoring Report*, https://lipor.pt/pt/a-lipor/o-negocio/economia-circular-residuo-como-recurso/. [4]

London Waste and Recycling Board (2017), *London's Circular Economy Route Map*, http://www.lwarb.gov.uk/wp-content/uploads/2015/04/LWARB-London%E2%80%99s-CE-route-map_16.6.17a_singlepages_sml.pdf (accessed on 5 August 2019). [16]

LWARB (2017), *Employment and the Circular Economy: Job Creation through Resource Efficiency in London*, http://www.wrap.org.uk (accessed on 29 January 2020). [11]

Mairie de Paris (2015), *White Paper on the Circular Economy of Greater Paris*, https://api-site.paris.fr/images/77050 (accessed on 11 June 2019). [17]

Morley, A., E. Looi and C. Zhao (2018), *Measuring the Circular Economy: Developing an Indicator Set for Opportunity Peterborough*. [2]

OECD (2015), *Stakeholder Engagement for Inclusive Water Governance*, OECD Studies on Water, OECD Publishing, Paris, https://dx.doi.org/10.1787/9789264231122-en. [6]

OECD (forthcoming), *The Circular Economy in Cities and Regions*, Synthesis Report, OECD Publishing, Paris. [5]

Organi Trust (2019), *Circular Economy and Organic Certification*, https://organitrust.org/ (accessed on 11 June 2019). [20]

Organising Committee of the Olympic and Paralympic Games Tokyo 2020 (2018), *Tokyo 2020 Olympic and Paralympic Games Sustainability Plan Version 2 (Draft)*. [15]

Region of Brussels (2016), *Brussels Region Regional Programme for the Circular Economy 2016-20*, https://www.circulareconomy.brussels/a-propos/le-prec/?lang=en (accessed on 21 February 2020). [22]

Umeå Municipality (2018), *EGCA 2018, Umeå, Sweden 7. Waste Production and Management 7A. Present Situation*. [26]

Urban Lab (2019), *Pourquoi l'Urban Lab ?*, https://urbanlab.parisandco.paris/Notre-offre/Pourquoi-l-Urban-Lab (accessed on 13 February 2020). [24]

Valladolid Municipality (2019), *Convocatoria pública de concesión de subvenciones para proyectos de fomento de economía circular y ecoinnovación y ecodiseño en el municipio de Valladolid en el Año 2019*. [27]

Vercalsteren, A., M. Christis and V. Van Hoof (2018), *Indicators for a Circular Economy*, Circular Flanders, https://vlaanderen-circulair.be/src/Frontend/Files/userfiles/files/Summa%20-%20Indicators%20for%20a%20Circular%20Economy.pdf. [3]

Zero Waste Scotland (2019), *Circular Economy in Cities and Regions*, https://www.zerowastescotland.org.uk/circular-economy/cities-and-regions (accessed on 6 November 2019). [23]

Annex A. Circular economy award-winning projects in 2017 and 2018

Sector	Institution	Project	Description	Year
Alternative energy	"Energética" Cooperative	KitSol	Development of a portable solar photovoltaic kit prototype by the Cooperative "Energética".	2017
	Spanish Association for Energy Recovery from Biomass (AVEBIOM)	Bioenergía	Promotion of the use of bioenergy as a source of sustainable and renewable energy in Valladolid. The project provides the keys to comply with legislation and disseminates information on energy market trends.	2017
Bio-economy	Guillermo Puerta Galván	Rescuing Flavours and Knowledge. A return to the origin.	Study on the potential for local production and consumption of traditional vegetable varieties.	2018
	Trovant technology	Obtaining biofertilisers from farming waste	Evaluation of the viability of obtaining biofertiliser by means of composting process from sheep manure.	2018
	UVE	ECOCIPienso, Circular Economy in the manufacture of animal feeds	Productive model in the agro-food industry based on the principles of the circular economy. It allows reducing the consumption and dependence on new natural resources outside the municipality and the region. The project aims at putting a value on organic waste, agro-food and plastics, and turning them into resources for other industries.	2018
Certifications and labels	EDUCA Valladolid Business Association	Circular Business Stamp	Development of a stamp certifying companies that carry out circular economy processes.	2018
Citizen participation	Belén Muñoz García	ValladolidColabora.com	Creation of an online platform for citizen collaboration. Citizens can send suggestions and complaints to the municipality through the platform.	2017
Eco-design	ABSOTEC, Acoustic Absorption	Eco-design of acoustic solutions (Eco Acoustics)	Redesign of products and acoustic solutions with the least material waste.	2018
	Innovative Business Cluster on Efficient Construction (AEICE)	HabitARTE	Eco-design contest for building equipment elements for collective use.	2018
	Institute for Development Promotion and Training (INFODEF)	EC Artisan sector	Introduction of the eco-design in the artisan sector. Training to artisan professors so that they can introduce eco-design contents in their academic curricula.	2017
	Saúl Alonso Pérez	CIC/LOC	Development of a prototype of a safe bicycle park following the parameters of eco-design.	2018
	Sexmo de Óvilo	EcoCONTAINER Lab	Centre for the development and innovation of biodegradable packaging prototype to facilitate the distribution to local micro-producers in online and retail markets.	2018
Energy management	BEFESA Aluminium	Use of energy as a fuel of a secondary stream of hydrogen obtained in the process of recovery of salt slag.	Use of recovered hydrogen as an alternative fuel to the natural gas (reduction of 20%) and to avoid CO_2 emissions per year.	2018

Sector	Institution	Project	Description	Year
Hospitality sector	Vallisoletan Hospitality Engineering	Recovery of materials from catering equipment for sale.	Promotion of the connection between the hospitality sector and various industries to implement innovative solutions to recover material from catering equipment for sale.	2018
	Vallisoletan Hospitality Engineering	Renting of equipment and machinery for the hotel/restaurant sector.	Provision of a rental service to companies in the hospitality and catering sector that allows the equipment to be kept longer in use, offering more competitive prices and minimising waste reduction.	2018
Mobility	José Ignacio Alonso Meneses	Converting conventional bicycles into electrically assisted bicycles.	Installation of electric engines on conventional bicycles as urban means of transport.	2018
	Sexmo de Óvilo	M.A.E. Movilidad Asistida EcoTURÍSTICA	Creation of a new touristic public transport service, promoting artisan and ecological production centres, offering routes and excursions for mini-groups with a guide on electric vehicles.	2018
Research, training and awareness-raising	3D printing Laboratory Kirolab	3D Printing	Use of recycled plastics for 3D printing processes.	2017
	Alpha Syltec Engineering	AR Vacircular	Application of Augmented Reality (AR) to promote citizen training in a circular economy through mobile applications, which will mix real and virtual elements.	2018
	BEFESA Aluminium	Study and improvement of the quality of the flux salts recovered from the salt slag valuation process.	Valuation process allows the recovery of the salts, returning them to the secondary aluminium foundries and thus constituting a closed cycle that avoids adding commercial salts of mineral origin and generates less energy consumption.	2018
	Business Project Management Solutions and Technologies	Successful Circular Economy Projects – PECExit	Project management training to increase the project's success probabilities and promote the efficient use of resources.	2018
	Digitel on trusted services	Blockchain platform for sustainable mobility	Research study to create a blockchain platform to improve air quality through sustainable mobility.	2018
	EDUCA Valladolid Business and Professionals Association	Educa auditing	Study on the circular economy in the business sector in Valladolid. The aim of the study is to offer guidance to companies in their circular transition. The institution is working on the creation of a circular certification and a code of good practices.	2017
	EFI HYGIENE S.L.U.	100% sustainable establishments with cradle-to-cradle cleaning products	Provision of training, dissemination and implementation of cradle-to-cradle certified cleaning products.	2018
Research, training and awareness-raising	EMPRENDENEXT	Circular Weekend	The Circular Weekend gathers start-ups and local projects participating in workshops and advice. Post-event mentoring sessions are organised for the best projects and ideas.	2017
	EMPRENDENEXT	Circular Weekend	Dissemination of working methodologies in the circular economy. Participants learn to launch circular ideas, convert existing business models to circular ones and get in touch with actors in various sectors.	2018
	Enviroo	ValladolidEScircular	Preparation of the report ValladolidEScircular. The document identified the 11 sectors in Valladolid with more potential for the circular economy.	2017
	Federation of Neighbourhood Associations of Valladolid "Antonio Machado"	Cultura Circular	Organisation of citizen awareness-raising campaigns towards sustainable consumption patterns, also for schools.	2017

Sector	Institution	Project	Description	Year
	Federation of Neighbourhood Associations of Valladolid "Antonio Machado"	Hogar Circular	Development of an itinerant kitchen module that can be installed in public spaces. Its goal is to raise awareness on circular cooking practices that can be applied in any kitchen on a daily basis.	2017
	Innovative Business Cluster on Efficient Construction (AEICE)	ECO Circular	Capacity-building activities on the circular economy for labour associations.	2017
Retail and manufacturing	Aromatics and essences del páramo	Essences of Valladolid	Valorisation of the remainders of urban lavender in order to obtain essential oil. The oil is used as a resource to produce hand soap and the residues are used as fertiliser-compost for gardens.	2018
	ARTENCANAL	Sofar Sound	Organisation of concerts in "circular" spaces created with recovered materials.	2017
	Biotechnology and Natural Resources Systems	Lanaland	Development of a model project of vegetable covers made from sheep wool.	2017
	Innovative Business Cluster on Efficient Construction (AEICE)	Ecocivil	Introduction of recycled aggregates in the construction sector.	2017
	Luis Miguel Benito Fraile (NEMORIS)	Reusable wine packaging	Research study that patented two prototypes of wine bottle cases that can be reused without intermediate manufacture as nest boxes for animals that feed themselves from insects.	2018
	Management Consultants and Technological Projects (CGPROTEC)	Digital and Circular Transformation of Kiosks	Renewal strategy based on the reuse of the network of kiosks that can contribute to the reduction of carbonisation due to the transport of parcels in cities.	2018
	Valladolid Swan Piragüismo Club	Circular kayaking	Four prototypes from obsolete kayaks for recreational activities.	2018
Retail and manufacturing	Ysolkrea S.L.N.E.	Pistachio "Green Beat"	Application of the circular economy to the pistachio production. The project aims to develop a cosmetic product from organic pistachio waste.	2017
	Ysolkrea S.L.N.E.	Development of a cosmetic product from organic pistachio residues.	Identification of the most suitable properties of the pistachio for the manufacture of eco-innovative cosmetic products.	2018
Waste management	3D printing Laboratory Kirolab	Replastic 3D	Introduction of recycled plastic materials and design of new recycled products.	2018
	ARTENCANAL	Recristal	Development of an action protocol for the reuse of old aluminium carpentry.	2017
	Biotechnology Resources Systems Natur	Compostero viajero	Extension of the practice of composting organic waste in schools and houses.	2018
	Biotechnology Resources Systems Natur	Recycling of food industry waste	Reuse of waste from the food industry, wheat bran and molasses from the sugar industry.	2018
	DYJ Iintegral Management (David Herrador Fernández)	Micro Reciclando	Creation of a transportable system of operative micro-recycling for the recycling of plastics, made up of four machines and carrying out demonstration days.	2018
	EDUCA Valladolid Business Association	Good practice platform	Web platform for exchanging experiences between companies committed to circular production models, connecting them with waste producers in order to use them as raw material.	2018

Sector	Institution	Project	Description	Year
	Juan Antonio Medina Cuaresma (Buteo Environmental Initiatives)	Madera que reVIVE	Use of wood waste to create biodiversity refuges for birds, insects and bats, promoting knowledge of urban biodiversity.	2017
	Paraje Innovation and Consultancy	Fungyble	Development of a system for the generation of biodegradable materials as an alternative to expanded polystyrene.	2017
	RDNEST	Sterling	Solution for the selective collection of waste that allows the measurement of the level of filling of the containers, identifies the user and recognises the user's credit for having used the containers.	2018
	SANDACH El Campillo	SANDACH El Campillo	SANDACH stands for Animal subproducts not intended for human consumption. It is based on a system of collection and separation of animal by-products not intended for human consumption in the Campillo market.	2017
	Villarramiel Consulting	Recovery and transformation of organic waste	Creation of a new business model based on the collection of waste generated by bars and restaurants in the city, waste treatment and transformation into materials that can be sold.	2018
Water management	I-CATALIST	IMPLUVIUM Project	Design of rainwater collection system in buildings. Reuse of water for irrigation of school and Durban gardens.	2017
	I-CATALIST	IMPLUVIUM Project	Development of a system that mitigates the risk of flooding in a public school, as well as the incorporation of a system of rainwater collection for irrigation of the existing school garden. The project is part of the IMPLUVIUM Project subsidised in 2017.	2018
	I-CATALIST	Closing the loop: Innovating in green and blue	Development of a board game for students, based on the implementation of different environment-related solutions (structural and non-structural) and on the Valladolid Water Cycle. The aim is to raise awareness on the benefits that green infrastructure can bring to the city on the basis of a set of possible sources of financing and business models.	2018
	TE Consulting House 4 Plus S.L.	Fangos EDAR	Study on the technical and economic viability of thermal hydrolysis processes in Valladolid's Wastewater Treatment Plant (EDAR). The project aims to increase the biogas production by 20% and use of Class A organic fertiliser from waste for agriculture.	2017
	Trovant Technology	Study of the potential for recovery of sewage sludge through co-digestion and conversion of bioplastics.	Evaluation of the viability and impact of bioplastics through biological processes from sludge in the context of EDAR Valladolid.	2018
	University School of Agricultural Engineering (INEA) Foundation	Refill, send a message with your bottle.	A new form and culture of plastic-free water in urban space through the implementation of a network of filling places with free and/or paid bulk water dispensers.	2018

Source: Own elaboration based on Valladolid Municipality, Circular Economy Project Promotion (2017, 2018).

Annex B. Evaluation criteria applied to select the winning-award projects in 2019

Evaluation criteria	Maximum score
1. Promotion of employment<ul><li>Generation of new employment and/or improvement of employment:<ul><li>For each new full-time permanent employment: 5 points.</li><li>For each new indefinite part-time employment: 3 points.</li><li>For each new full-time temporary employment: 0.2 points for each month of the contract.</li><li>For each new temporary employment part-time employment: 0.1 points for each month of the contract.</li><li>For job improvement: 1.5 points.</li></ul></li></ul>	20
2. Economic and social aspects<ul><li>Projects that contribute to the creation of business opportunities in the municipality of Valladolid, which allow the economic development of the city and its contextual environment, and are technically, environmentally and economically viable.</li><li>Level of simplicity for the integration of the proposed project/activity in the value chain of the current economic activities of Valladolid (e.g. availability of raw materials, manufacture of products and its components, repair, recycling companies, etc.).</li><li>Positive assessment of the relevance of the social nature of the project (e.g. insertion of workers at risk of inclusion, social minorities, etc.).</li></ul>	12
3. Technical and/or methodological quality<ul><li>Degree of elaboration, detail and coherence of the work plan, schedule and activities with the planned objectives.</li><li>Definition of adequate and sufficient performance indicators and monitoring and measurement mechanisms to assess the effectiveness of the proposed measures before and after their implementation.</li><li>Quality/price ratio, with an adequate justification of the requested budget for the different activities.</li><li>Potential for actions and impact on the business of the sector.</li></ul>	9
4. Environmental sustainability<ul><li>Projects that ensure the maximisation of environmental benefits, expressed in the relevant units (e.g. minimisation of waste generation, avoided atmospheric emissions, saving of raw materials, etc.).</li><li>Projects with a full or partial Product Life Cycle approach: Generation of raw materials, design, production, distribution, consumption, collection and/or recycling.</li><li>Positive assessment of companies or organisations that have an environmental management system, seal or environmental badge, as well as those whose main activity belongs to the environmental sector.</li><li>Renewable energy use: Energy efficiency, reduction in resource consumption, renewable resources, resources with low environmental impact, emission reduction, recyclable and/or energy reusable products.</li><li>Development of actions based on nature.</li></ul>	16
5. Eco-innovation<ul><li>Consideration of the state of the art of the technology or methodology used; Approach to the use of the best available technique and best environmental practice.</li><li>Degree of novelty and potential to become an innovation.</li><li>Positive assessment of entities with a recognition of their innovative nature.</li></ul>	8

Evaluation criteria	Maximum score
6. Eco-design - Durable, low maintenance, timeless and/or modular products. - Existence of an eco-label, related to potentially certifiable products. Design of implementation and certification strategy. - Information on recycled materials. - 3D layout. - Estimation of investment/tangible benefits. - Creation and development of a prototype and its validation.	12
7. Quantitative/qualitative scope of impact - Assessment of the scope of the proposed measures in quantitative or qualitative terms (e.g. people served, estimated billing, degree of specialisation), valuing positively the projects of greater scope. - Assessment of impacts on the water footprint, energy consumption, carbon footprint and waste production.	7
8. Diversification of supports - Support for different activities within the four categories proposed in the call, seeking diversity within the economic landscape of the municipality. - Support for projects within the different industrial or service sectors, which are considered a priority for the Municipality: transport, bio-economy, eco-industry, waste, agro-food, energy, water and the public sector.	8
9. Priority products - Plastics and bioplastics. - Food waste. - Textile. - Rubber.	5

Note: In case of a tie in the global scores, priority would be given to the score obtained in section 1 of the evaluation criteria (Employment Promotion). If the tie persists, the score obtained in section 4 of the evaluation criteria would be prioritised (Environmental Relevance). If the tie still continues, the entry date of the application in the register (considering the date and time), would be taken into account.

Source: Valladolid Municipality (2019), *Convocatoria pública de concesión de subvenciones para proyectos de fomento de economía circular y ecoinnovación y ecodiseño en el municipio de Valladolid en el Año 2019*.

Annex C. List of stakeholders consulted during the policy dialogue

Institution	Name
AEICE (Innovative Business Cluster on Efficient Construction)	Enrique Cobreros García
AEICE (Innovative Business Cluster on Efficient Construction)	Carmen Devesa Fernández
Aquavall	José María de Cuenca
AVADECO (Valladolid Trade Association)	María Balsa Carrasco
BE Circular/Provincial Association of Hospitality Entrepreneurs of Valladolid/Circular Culture	Beatriz Quintana
Business Confederation of Valladolid (CVE)	Noemí García
CARTIF Foundation	Dolores Hidalgo
Chamber of Commerce, Industry and Services of Valladolid	Ana Atienza Pérez
CIDAUT Foundation	Maite Fernández Peña
CyLog Association	Cristina Laredo Olivera
Duero Hydrographic Confederation (CHD)	Ignacio Rodríguez Muñoz
ECOEMBES - Valladolid/Circular Lab	Alberto Fernández
ECOEMBES - Valladolid/Circular Lab	Isabel Tennenbaum Casado
Ecomarketing/Circular Culture/Pistachios Green Beat	Javier Rodríguez Conte
EDUCA (Valladolid Business and Professionals Association)	Maribel Barrante
Energética Cooperative	Juan Carlos Zamora
Enviroo - Emprendenext	Agustín Valentín-Gamazo Villar
FECOSVA (Trade and Services Federation of Valladolid and Province)	Milagros Aguado Mariscal
FECOSVA (Trade and Services Federation of Valladolid and Province)	Victor Muñoz
Federation of Neighbourhood Associations of Valladolid "Antonio Machado"	Margarita García Álvarez
FOACAL-CEARCAL (Federation of Handicraft Organisations)	Felix Sanz
General Union of Workers (UGT)	Nuria González Escudero
INEA University School	Andrés Gómez Diez
INEA Foundation	María Antonia González Varela
INEA Foundation	Dunia Virto González
INFODEF (Institute for Development Promotion and Training)	Jesus Boyano Sierra
Institute of Foreign Trade (ICEX)	Miguel Angel Garrido
INTRAS Foundation	Eva Iglesias
Juan Soñador Foundation	David Castro Vega
Michelin	Hugo Ureta Alonso
Ministry for Ecological Transition and Demographic Challenge (MITECO)	Carmen Durán Vizán
Natural Heritage Foundation (JCYL-FPN) - Castile and León	Jesus Díez
Natural Heritage Foundation (JCYL-FPN) - Castile and León	Sara Delgado
Official College of Engineers (COIIM-Valladolid)	Carlos J. Moreno Montero

Institution	Name
Provincial Hospitality Association	María José de la Calle
Renault	Mario Cardeñoso
School of Industrial Organisation	Eva Curto
Spanish Federation of Municipalities and Provinces (FEMP)	Luis Enrique Mecati Granado
University of Valladolid (UVa)	Gonzalo Parrado Hernando
Valladolid Municipality - Agency of Innovation and Economic Development	Jesús Gómez Pérez
Valladolid Municipality - Agency of Innovation and Economic Development	Ana Isabel Page Polo
Valladolid Municipality - Agency of Innovation and Economic Development	Gloria San José Fernández
Valladolid Municipality - Agency of Innovation and Economic Development	Alicia Villazan
Valladolid Municipality - Conservation Centre	Jesus Briones
Valladolid Municipality - Culture and Tourism Department (Culture)	Ana Isabel Boillos Rubio
Valladolid Municipality - Environment and Sustainability Department (Executive Secretariat)	Cristina Raymundo
Valladolid Municipality - Environment and Sustainability Department (Municipal Energy Agency)	María José Ruiz de Villa
Valladolid Municipality - Environment and Sustainable Development Department (Waste)	Javier Ruiz Monge
Valladolid Municipality - Innovation, Economic Development, Employment and Commerce Department	Rosa Huertas González
Valladolid Municipality - Health and Security Department (Municipal Cleaning service)	Andrés Herguedas García
Valladolid Municipality - Health and Security Department	Miguel Sancho
Valladolid Municipality – Mobility Department	Roberto Riol
Valladolid Municipality – Mobility Department	Ignacio Sánchez
Valladolid Municipality – Urban Space Department	Francisco Andrés Pérez Nieto
VITARTIS (Agro-food Industry Cluster)	Gema Belén Prieto Jiménez
Workers Commissions (CCOO)	Cristina de la Torre
Workers Commissions (CCOO)	Gonzalo Franco Blanco

www.ingramcontent.com/pod-product-compliance
Lightning Source LLC
LaVergne TN
LVHW061944070526
838199LV00060B/3963